Letters to a
Young Life Leader

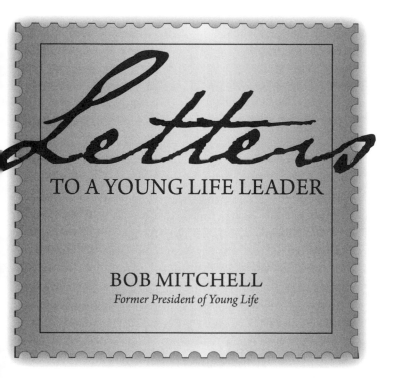

Letters

TO A YOUNG LIFE LEADER

BOB MITCHELL
Former President of Young Life

Whitecaps Media
HOUSTON

Whitecaps Media
Houston, Texas
whitecapsmedia.com

Bob Mitchell may be contacted through the publisher's website.

ISBN: 978-0-9836825-7-8

SECOND PRINTING

For information on bulk purchases of this book, please visit whitecapsmedia.com

Printed in the United States of America

Table of Contents

SECTION FOUR
— FINALLY … —

P. S.
— SPIRITUAL FORMATION —

To all those leaders
who care for young people
enough to go where they are,
making friends with them,
and leading them into the magnificent
journey of faith and love found only in Jesus

Foreword

"The best Young Life work has yet to be done."

That was an encouragement Jim Rayburn, Young Life's founder, often gave to the early staff of the ministry.

No one has ever had—or will ever have again—the vantage point of Young Life that Bob Mitchell has had. From his days as one of Rayburn's original "club kids" through his years as President of Young Life and his current involvement with leaders around the world, "Mitch" has been intimately involved with the mission on every possible level. Not a single day has passed since 1940 that Young Life hasn't been on his mind.

When it comes to Young Life, you have the advantage of youth. Your closeness to the kids of today as well as your creativity and energy are wonderful gifts that God has given you to impact this ministry.

Mitch, no longer young at eighty-three, has the advantage of age. His wisdom stems from almost seven decades of walking closely with Christ. That wisdom, coupled with insights into Young Life born out of his unique perspective, makes him the ideal person to address the essential issues of what it means to be a Young Life leader.

Our hope is that this book will help combine youth and age, new and old, to help prove Jim Rayburn's admonition: The best Young Life work is yet to be done, and you—coupled with the principles Mitch shares in this book—are just the ones to do it!

—KIT SUBLETT, EDITOR

Introduction

Dear Young Life Leaders,

I am writing these letters to you because I know I must! I'm eighty-three now, and partially blind, but, thank the Lord, still able to function well enough to share my heart with you, and to offer prayers and support for your ministry.

You may be a Young Life staff person, or a volunteer leader, or a committee person, or a donor. You may be a youth pastor or church volunteer. Leadership takes many forms. A leader is one who influences others through the power of his or her person and gifting.

One thing we have in common ... we know for sure that kids in our broken world need to hear about Jesus, and be given the opportunity to trust him with their lives!

Young Life has been about this life-giving mission since 1940. What a wonderful journey it has been! I have been privileged to be part of it since its very beginning in Dallas, Texas, where I was born and grew up. Over the years I have been a club kid, a Campaigner kid, a volunteer leader, a committee person, a field staff person, an Area Director, a Regional Director, a Divisional Director, the Mission Training Director, the U.S. Field Director, the President of Young Life, and the President of the Young Life Foundation. In addition, I have enjoyed countless leadership positions in Young Life's tremendous year-round camping ministry. Now, in these "golden years" my wife, Claudia, and I often are privileged to speak and teach throughout this wonderful worldwide mission community.

I think I know the wide range of feelings you have as you engage in this ministry with kids. I have "been there ... done that!" In these letters I will not dance around the issues, or hide the failures and discouragements, along with the unbelievable moments of joy and fulfillment of purpose! Please know that my main reason for writing these letters is to encourage you in your faith journey. Along with that, please allow me to teach some basic principles for leadership that I believe have withstood the test of time—things that must not be lost as the years continue!

In the days of the steam locomotive this story was told. It seems that somewhere in the South a dog was being shipped by train. For a couple of days the dog sat in its crate on the station platform. Finally someone asked the station attendant about the dog and its destination. He answered, "We don't know what we're gonna do with that dog. He don't know where it is he come from, and he don't know where it is he's a-goin' ... and furthermore, he done chewed up his tag!"

It's important to know "where it is we come from and where it is we're a-goin.'" I know there are those who would say that "history," or, from where it is that Young Life has come, is not important. Not wishing to dwell in the past, they would insist, "What is past is past! What is now is now!" I understand this thinking and the desire to "move on," and not attempt to recapture feelings of the good old days.

But we ignore our history to our peril! To "chew up the tag" of important lessons learned, the ways God has led, may mean that we will be less effective in our mission, and tragically, we may even repeat our mistakes. God forbid that we forget those leadings from him which are timeless and essential!

I have no desire to dwell in the past, and I celebrate today the obvious growth and influence of Young Life in the United States and the world. You are involved in a most remarkable ministry with young people—perhaps the greatest of its kind the world has ever seen!

In my letters I shall tell stories. These are part of the Young Life history. Hopefully, they will help you to understand present day realities, and why we do what we do. I am in good company here. Jesus, with his disciples, often would teach right out of the biblical history of God's chosen people.

Boil everything down and Young Life begins and continues because of the greatest event in all of human history—nothing comes close in comparison. It is the story of Jesus. God came here in human flesh. He lived his perfect life among us. By looking at him we can see what God is like.

On the cross he died to forgive all of sinful humankind. His resurrection assures us of our eternity with him. Through his Spirit he continues to live his life in us in our broken world. And he will come again to receive us to himself forever.

The first verses I memorized as one of Jim Rayburn's original Campaigner kids were 1 John 5:11–12. "And this is the testimony: God has given us eternal life, and this life is in his Son. He who has the Son has life; he who does not have the Son of God does not have life."

This is the absolute heart and core of Young Life: *Jesus Christ is life!*

It is imperative that we as leaders devote ourselves to communicating powerfully this message to kids. What are they hearing and feeling when we speak to them? Do they sense our overwhelming love and commitment to the person of Jesus?

When Jim spoke to us in that first Young Life club, "Club 37," which met in my home, he was masterful in reliving with us the stories of Jesus in the Gospels. I have never heard anyone so gifted. But probably what captivated us was his passion. We knew that down deep he believed and felt every word he said!

Nothing in all the world is more important than what you are doing! I hope that deep in your heart you believe that!

Years ago a statement was made from Vatican II, a world mission conference: "The future of humanity lies in the hands of those strong enough to give future generations reasons for living, and for hoping!"

That is what you are about! You are giving young people reasons for living and for hoping … as can only be found in Jesus Christ and his purposes throughout the world! I'm so thankful for you, and I wish to stand with you in your wonderful journey! I'll stay in touch. You are in my prayers.

God bless you!

—BOB MITCHELL
Monument, Colorado
Summer 2012

Section One

— Roots —

*S*hoots and *S*queezuns

This book has four sections, each with several letters about a general topic; those sections are then followed by a fifth section, the world's longest postscript. I will introduce each section not with a letter, but with a story. It seems like a good place to begin would be my own story.

When I was growing up, as my family sat around the dinner table, each of us reported on the events of our day. We were a small family—Mom and Dad, my brother, two years older, and me.

When it was Dad's turn one night in 1940, he told us about a meeting he had that day at the factory with a young seminary student who had come in asking for money. The factory was a family-owned machinery manufacturing business, the John E. Mitchell Company, founded by my grandfather. My father Orville was Vice-President in charge of manufacturing and my Uncle John was President. Other relatives occupied various positions in the company. The business was successful and well-known in Dallas as a major employer, and for its philanthropic history. People often came in to request donations for their various causes, especially for youth programs. They knew how much the family loved kids. Uncle John taught a large high school Sunday school class at First Presbyterian Church, and Dad was Scoutmaster, and an Eagle Scout himself, for the largest troop in Dallas, Troop 55, with over one hundred boys active in the troop.

As Dad related his story I could tell there was something very special about this meeting with the young seminarian, whose name was Jim Rayburn. It seems that Jim wanted to reach Dallas teenagers with the gospel of Jesus, especially those young people who had no regular connection with the church, who were on the outside, and were either indifferent or hostile to the faith. At the time this was a large percentage of kids in Dallas, whether it was about Protestant, Catholic, or Jewish worship.

Rayburn's idea was to hold a tent campaign for kids of the Dallas high schools. Tent meetings were pretty common in the South in those days, but never were they designed primarily to reach teenage kids who were distant from the faith. Recently Jim had held a similar and successful campaign in the nearby town of Gainesville, and he thought it would work in the large city of Dallas, so he came to my father and uncle to ask for money to rent a circus tent for a week.

I remember blurting out that evening at the table, "Well, did you give him the money?" It seemed like a pretty far-out idea to me, and I thought about my own friends and how they might respond to a religious deal like that.

Dad said, "Yes, we did. I've never met anyone like this young man—or anyone who has such a passion for kids."

I had no idea that in this very moment of history I was witnessing the birth of one of the most remarkable ministries to young people the world has ever known. It was through this mission that countless thousands of kids the world over would experience their own personal introduction to Jesus Christ, and that I too would come to faith.

Weeks later the campaign began. The tent was set up right across from Fair Park. Most every kid in Dallas knew this location, having been to the Texas State Fair, or to games in the Cotton Bowl.

A huge sign was set in front of the tent: "YOUNG LIFE CAMPAIGN — HEAR JIM RAYBURN!" (Jim had heard the name, "Young Life," used for a youth program in Great Britain, and had asked permission to use it in his campaigns. This also is the origin of the name given to Young Life's Christian nurture groups, "Campaigners.")

There had been a lot of publicity in the two Dallas papers. A few churches got behind the campaign, with some of their kids getting the word out to their schoolfriends.

Workers from the Mitchell Company, only a few blocks away, had come to build wooden benches, a speakers' platform, and a choir platform for a high school choir which had been rehearsing for the event.

Almost eight hundred kids came out that first night, along with a sprinkling of adults. As the week went on the crowds grew to over a thousand, overflowing the tent. Benches were hastily constructed and placed outside.

My family was part of the crowd. As best I know this was the first time I really heard the gospel story, to take it personally, as did my brother. In later years my mother and father would look back upon that week in the tent as a vital turning point in their faith journeys as well.

There was an upbeat feel to the meetings. Jim's brother, Bob, played one piano, and Howard Kee, a student at Dallas Theological Seminary, a second one. Both were accomplished musicians. The choir was superb, and, as I remember, had in it some very good looking girls (for this reason, my friends and I always sat up toward the front!).

This was just prior to the Second World War and the national mood was very patriotic. We sang with enthusiasm patriotic/religious songs like,

> *What though wars may come*
> *with marching feet, and beat of the drum*
> *for I have Christ in my heart.*
> *What though nations rage*
> *as we approach the end of the age*
> *for I have Christ in my heart …*

And also,

> *On the land, on the sea*
> *in the air, He watches over me.*
> *Over here, over there, anywhere*
> *my Father watches over me.*
> *For whether it be at the battle front with bursting bomb or shell*
> *or whether it be at home or abroad the words of life to tell …*
> *On the land, on the sea, in the air,*
> *my Father watches over me!*

By far the most powerful moment each night was when Jim stood before us to proclaim Jesus. I had never heard anything like it! Our family, like many in the South, was churchgoing. But I knew very little about the wonders and implications of the Incarnation—that God, in Jesus, became flesh and dwelt among us!

To this day, I remember vividly Jim's first talk. I had never heard anyone speak like that! Holding his New Testament in his hands, he walked through the story of John 2, the wedding in Cana, when Jesus changed the water into wine. We were there ... captivated ... right in the story! Jim took us there, as so often he did in subsequent years with other stories of Jesus.

Jim opened his Bible to John 2, where a social catastrophe had occurred. People in charge had run out of wine during a wedding party. Mary, the mother of Jesus, told him of this crisis. Jesus instructed the servants to fill six twenty-gallon water jars with water. These jars were used in the Jewish ritual of foot washing. Then Jesus told the servants to dip some out from the jars and give a drink to the master of ceremonies, which they did. The water had become excellent wine, and the master of ceremonies was astounded. This first miracle of Jesus, as recorded by John, revealed Jesus as the Creator, and his disciples believed in him.

Here's what I remember of Jim's talk. It went something like this ... "Do you know how to make wine? (Of course, we didn't, but it sounded interesting.) Well, first you must have just the right soil. Then you plant a shoot, or cutting. Pretty soon you have a vine. Then there comes grapes on the vine. You pick the grapes and mash them, to make squeezuns out of them. Then you let the squeezuns sit around a long time in a barrel or something. Then after all that, you have wine. It just works that way."

What a fabulous communication style we heard that night! To this day I can hear Jim exaggerate the word, *squeezuns*, saying it over and over in his characteristic Texas drawl. Every time I hear someone speak, or speak myself, from this text, I think of the "squeezuns," and I hear Jim's voice once again.

Continuing, he said, "But you know, Jesus didn't have any soil, or any shoots, or any vines, or any grapes, or any squeezuns. And it only took him a few minutes to accomplish this miracle.

He just took some old brackish West Texas well water in some foot-washing jugs and turned it into the best wine there ever was!

"And you know what? That's what he will do with your life, if you let him! He'll take whatever you are, common and ordinary, messed up and not very perfect, in fact, maybe even smelly ... and he will make your life into something wonderful that others will celebrate and enjoy forever! He did it with foot-washing water, and he will do it with you, if you will invite him into your life! Right now, you can say to Jesus, 'Please, Lord, give me that life. I want to be one of your disciples!'"

Then the choir sang,

> *If you'll take my Jesus while he's passing by.*
> *If you'll take my Jesus he'll sure satisfy.*
> *If you'll take my Jesus he'll hear your heart's cry.*
> *If you'll take my Jesus tonight.*

This most likely is the week when I opened my life to the Savior, and became a follower of Jesus. Only God knows when anyone truly comes to faith. But for me, life would never be the same. I joined brothers and sisters all over the world, in every nation, to love Jesus and proclaim his eternal message of forgiveness, transformation, and hope. Thanks be to God!

In this section of letters I will reflect on some of our founding essentials, as they are still vital today.

"Where's your Bible?"

Dear Young Life Leader,

The early leaders started meeting with kids in Dallas who had become followers of Jesus. They called these groups "Campaigners." The name came from the early tent meetings which were called the "Young Life Campaign." Our group of boys met at Jim Rayburn's home on Sunday afternoons. There were no refreshments. The meetings had a "down to business" feel about them. For two hours we each gave a weekly report on our assignments, studied Scripture, memorized Bible verses, and learned to pray.

The same things went on in the girls' Campaigners groups, led by Gladys Roche, Ollie Dustin, Kay McDonald, Wanda Ann Mercer, or Anne Cheairs, some of the first women to join the Young Life staff. These women, and many others, would be legendary in their contribution to the mission.

In those early years an informal partnership was established with another ministry just being formed in California which had the purpose of Christian nurture for believers. Dawson Trotman had this vision, particularly for men in the military services of our country, many of whom served during the Second World War. This ministry was called The Navigators and it exists worldwide today, headquartered in Colorado Springs.

Jim and Daws were good friends, and the natural result was for the Navigators to shape significantly the way Young Life conducted its Campaigners programs. "Discipline" was the name of the game. We had "check-up" each week to see how we were doing in the various memory programs, prayer requirements, Bible study, and "witnessing" to our non-Christian friends.

One day Daws was visiting Jim from California and he came to our Campaigner group. Some of us who had met him before were pretty scared of him, even though we respected him very much. He had a most direct style that was intimidating to us kids. We got to the part of the meeting that day when we were to study the Bible. Everyone pulled out their New Testaments or Bibles—but, to my dismay, I had forgotten mine. Of course he noticed, and in his direct way Daws asked me, in front of everyone, "Where's your Bible?" For sure, I never forgot my Bible again for any Campaigners meeting!

The mission of Young Life has its roots in the Scriptures. Its method and message are biblical in their essence and practice. I believe this to be a major reason for the effectiveness and power in what you do with kids.

Over the years when I have stood before kids in a club or camp to proclaim the gospel I have felt uniquely privileged— like a person standing on holy ground! Who am I to join the prophets of old to proclaim, "This is what the Lord says!" I can't tell you how many times I cried out to the Father for the power of his Holy Spirit, once again to speak the message of Jesus through the Scripture and even through my words!

Let me ask you now the same question that I was asked a generation ago, "Where's your Bible?" Do you hold it in your hand, but also is it in your mind and heart? Are the Scriptures an everyday-guide to who you are, and how you live out your faith in a needy world? Are you reading and memorizing the words of Holy Scripture? Are you praying the Scriptures? Do kids see how important is the Word of God to you?

There is nothing more important than your love for Jesus— and one of the places that we must go to find him is the Bible. Don't neglect this.

In Christ,

Mitch

— Letter 2 —

Prayer is the Work

Dear Leader,

Many of you have heard stories about "the old days" and how much time we spent in prayer. Well, I'm here to tell you those stories are mostly true. We really did pray a lot. It wasn't all that romantic, a lot of it was born out of desperation. We were always running behind on our salaries and the only place we knew to go to was God himself. He always provided.

Much of this emphasis on prayer came from Jim, of course. In those early days he prayed more than anyone I had ever seen. When I was a young single staff guy, I lived at Star Ranch, our first property, which also served as Young Life's headquarters and the Rayburns' home. You could count every night on Jim praying long into the night. (Jim was a night person. I knew this because I often travelled with him and knew his patterns; I almost always saw him studying the Scriptures and praying into the wee hours of the night. I should add that Jim would wake up later in the day than the rest of us. Being the "Boss," he could get away with that.)

The next day he would tell us, "I just had a wonderful night with Jesus in prayer," and he would share with us insights he had received that night. Some were out of his Bible reading, some just what he sensed the Lord telling him.

It is fair to say that Young Life was bathed in prayer in those early years. "Prayer *is* the work," Jim would remind us.

One of the most well-known examples of our prayer life in those days were the times when Jim would call the staff men (women were not invited until much later) to Frontier for a few days of prayer as the fiscal year ended. We would pray around the clock for about three days, almost always because the mission was in a tough financial spot. Without fail, God came through.

Please don't think we were super-human or some sort of spiritual giants. One time I recall we were all kind of half asleep and we were talking to the Lord about things we were really ashamed of. One of the young staff men—a guy named Van Nall—confessed to the Lord that he had gotten so desperate for income that, rather than waiting on the Lord, he had started to raise chickens on the side and sell them.

As Van was saying that, a fellow by the name of Art Rech was nodding off and just heard Van confess something about chickens. It was Art's turn to pray next and when he did he prayed, "Lord, forgive Van for *stealing* those chickens." Well, that broke up the meeting as we all cracked up!

I am sorry to say that I didn't always live up to that pattern of fervent prayer as the years went on. But, as I will discuss in a future letter to you, I rediscovered the importance of prayer anew in my later years.

I love the activity of the mission of Young Life, and I love the activists that are in our ministry. You're doing things with kids that are of eternal consequence. Nothing could be more important than the direct ministry with kids you are doing! Except for one thing: Are you doing it out of an intimacy with Jesus in prayer? If not, I really worry. All of our activity must flow out of that intimacy.

Jesus said it so well, "Apart from me you can do nothing ... If you remain in me and my words remain in you, ask whatever you wish, and it will be given you" (John 15:5, 7). Do we understand that *that* is the mission of Young Life? It flows out of abiding with Christ, and you cannot do that without prayer, and lots of it.

Don't ever forget—prayer *is* the work!

Sincerely in Christ,

Mitch

Building Relationships With Those "Outside"

Dear Leader,

Let's look at two verses of Scripture which have been especially foundational in the mission of Young Life. Both are found in the writings of the Apostle Paul. They help us to understand our "roots," and why we do what we do.

First Thessalonians 4:12—". . . so that your daily life may win the respect of outsiders . . ."

Colossians 4:5—"Be wise in the way you act toward outsiders; make the most of every opportunity . . ."

Both verses refer to "outsiders." These are people outside the faith—people who don't know Jesus. These texts helped define for the first staff and Board what was to be the primary mission of Young Life. *It was to build relationships of love and trust with young people who were on the outside, sharing with them the gospel of Jesus Christ, and inviting them to believe and follow him.* These were kids who were non-believers, and usually non-churched kids. Obviously, some would be hard to reach. It would take time and much prayer to build relationships with them, but that was our mandate!

When Young Life began in the early 1940s, the term "outsiders" described accurately the majority of high school young people in the United States. Young Life, first and foremost, was to be an outreach ministry with those kids. Hopefully, this describes the Young Life we see today!

In past years when I was on staff there were times when we drifted from our calling to reach hard-to-reach kids for Jesus Christ, and found ourselves mostly involved in things that made the numbers impressive—like getting more kids to camp. Any time something like this happened, when we became numbers-oriented, we ran the risk of switching from being a mission community to being an organization or corporation, mostly interested in the bottom line.

At the end of a week of camp often there is a "Say-So" meeting when kids are given the opportunity to express that they came to faith in Jesus. I have been in some of these when well over half of those who spoke talked about rededicating their lives to Jesus. Only a few said, "I met Jesus this week." Of course we celebrate anyone coming closer to the Lord, but Young Life exists to be an outreach movement for young people who don't have any relationship with God. External pressure to make the numbers look good may mean "filling busses," and "meeting quotas," rather than reaching out to kids who need to know Jesus Christ.

Of course we wish for as many kids as possible to hear the good news of the gospel, and we will work hard to that end. But the shift to a performance orientation can be very subtle. We may not even be aware of inner changes in our motivation.

Reaching the "outsiders" will require much more than providing a good program of club and camp activities for them. The ministry must be "incarnational." That means going where kids are, seeking to understand their culture. We must build relationships of love and trust. Jesus, "the Word become flesh," did exactly that. He personally entered our broken world to show forth the love of God. Now he asks us to continue his incarnation with kids the world over.

All of this can only happen out of our own intimacy with Jesus. We must ask ourselves some essential questions ... How well do we know him? Are we men and women of prayer and reflection? Are we persons who allow his life to live in us through his Holy Spirit? Are we seeking to learn and grow in the Scriptures? Are we letting him love kids through us? This is where the power is. I'll say more about these things in future letters. In the meantime, keep at it—keep going after and loving those kids who are "outside" the Christian faith.

I'll stay in touch—

Mitch

— Letter 4 —

"Winning the Right to Be Heard"

Dear Leader,

There is a concept of ministry that has been basic to Young Life from its beginning. This is what is called, "winning the right to be heard." A simple explanation of this principle is that the one who proclaims the gospel is the same one who has spent much time with kids, being *with* them to establish credibility and trust. These people are effective in proclaiming the gospel, not as professional speakers, but as friends. We might call this Christian "withness."

This is true in every area of Young Life, not just the work in the local area. The other day we asked our oldest son, Tucker, what he remembers about growing up in Young Life, and especially spending much of each summer at a Young Life camp property while his father was camp director. He said he loved those summers, and then he made some rather profound observations.

He talked about the proclamation of the gospel that he heard over the years. He observed that the proclamation was given by leaders who had climbed mountains with the kids, who had done crazy skits that put themselves down, and who had hung out with the kids around camp. Speakers had the attention of campers because they had been with them to establish credibility and trust.

Effective Young Life leaders will be vulnerable and honest, not trying to be someone he or she is not. They will not be afraid of being ordinary. They will proclaim the gospel as those who have "won the right to be heard."

The purpose for what we call "contact work" is here also. As leaders we work hard to learn names. We go where kids are, and we seek to establish unconditional friendships with these young people.

I once heard a great quote by J. B. Phillips: "Jesus will not allow true religion to exist in comfortable little circles all its own. Real love demands action. It may mean coping at firsthand with the difficult, the unpleasant, and the messy." This is another way of saying, "winning the right to be heard."

When we look at the life of Jesus we learn that he did not live in isolated comfort, but walked each day with his disciples. He encountered people in great need. He dealt with religious fanatics. He truly was here on earth as God Incarnate. And if ever there was one who "won the right to be heard," it is Jesus!

I know what it feels like to look at a school full of kids whom we have never met. We wish to share the good news of the gospel with them, but the task seems overwhelming. I join with you to call out to God, as did the father of a demon-possessed son, "Lord, I believe; help thou mine unbelief!" (Luke 9:24, KJV).

Through the mystery of his Holy Spirit, he will enable you to *win the right to be heard*! May you be encouraged!

Mitch

In All You Do

Dear Leader,

Once again, I send my greetings. I hope you are encouraged with how things are going.

Given all that is involved in being a Young Life leader, and having been there myself for many years, I assure you, I know what it feels like:

To be a volunteer leader, spending hours around kids and their activities, and going to club and Campaigners, while still trying to do a decent job with your own family, your work, or your schoolwork ...

To receive a staff assignment in a city or town unfamiliar to you ...

To look at a school, while sitting in your car praying, "Lord, where do we begin?" ...

To drive to club wondering if anyone will show up ...

To be given from God your first committee person, who becomes your lifelong friend ...

To lose one of your best volunteers because of a move ...

To have your first kid come up after club or camp and say, "I met Jesus!" ...

To hear a Campaigner kid quote perfectly, John 3:16 ...

To go with parents to the local jail to bail out their kid …

To work in a hardcore inner city school or neighborhood …

To try to fill a bus for camp …

To have your first camp assignment …

To give your first gospel message in a club …

To make a call on a local pastor …

To try to be a good parent to your own kids …

To wonder if you can support your family financially …

To promote a Young Life banquet in your area …

To face a budget shortfall …

To receive affirmation from someone who matters very much to you …

To face your own spiritual dryness …

To be asked to give the local high school baccalaureate address …

To sit in a camp "Say-So" meeting and hear the kids you brought confess their faith in Jesus …

To receive a thank-you letter from a former club kid who now is a missionary in another country …

To celebrate another leader's success even though you are struggling …

(There is a story behind each of these personal experiences! The list could go on!)

Hang in there, and remember, this is not your ministry to accomplish, but rather is about Jesus doing his wonderful and eternal work in and through you—all through the great mystery of the Holy Spirit!

God bless you,

Mitch

Section Two

— Why? —

A Woman Speaker

Traditionally in Young Life the proclamation of the gospel message in a club or camp was always given by male leaders. That's just the way it was. A lot of it was a cultural thing, yet having some obscure connection with theological reasoning. For years I never questioned this rule, until one day in 1959.

After first serving on staff in Colorado, Claudia and I were by then living in the San Francisco Bay Area. We loved those days, and the ministry was flourishing. Clubs were big and hundreds of kids were going to camp each summer. The club I led, Acalanes High School, in Lafayette, usually had over a hundred kids in attendance. It seemed we were on a roll!

We had eight leaders helping us out. Staff woman Anne Cheairs looked after the women leaders, and she met regularly in training sessions and Bible studies with them. "Annie," as she was called, was one of the first staff members, working with Jim in the early years of Young Life in Texas. I knew her when I was in high school; she was a leader in my Young Life club, or "Club 37" as we called it. Annie was truly a great leader!

One day on a Tuesday evening as I was hurrying to get to club I got stuck in the Orinda tunnel, coming from Oakland. There had been a bad accident and traffic was going nowhere. In one hour the Acalanes club was scheduled to begin. Long before cell phones, there was no way for me to contact the other leaders to apprise them of my situation. All I could do was pray.

I had been doing a club message series on "The Seven Signs," or miracles, of Jesus in the Gospel of John, and was about halfway through the series. I was worrying about what would happen if I didn't show up to give my well-prepared club talk.

By the time the tunnel opened up it was too late for me to make it to club. I arrived there just as the kids were leaving, and learned that everything had gone very well. When Annie had seen that I was not going to make it to club, and when the time came for the club talk, she got up with her Bible and, with no preparation, gave the message on the next "sign" in the Gospel of John. Everyone said it was superb, and the kids loved it.

But how could that be? She was a woman!

Annie was quite traditional, and was reluctant to give talks, such as the one she gave that evening, but whenever I could get her to do it after that night, she was great, mostly because she knew the Scriptures so well, and loved Jesus so much! The kids recognized the living presence of the Lord in her, and that's what mattered most!

I was beginning my life-changing journey toward understanding the role of women in all forms of leadership in Young Life. Fortunately, my contemporaries and I were learning to ask the "Why?" question—in this particular case, the question, "Why do we only allow men to speak at club?" I'll talk about the specific issue of women in leadership in a later letter. For now, though, I want to introduce this important subject of knowing *why* we do the things we do.

Organizations will be in danger of losing their way if from time to time they do not ask the question, *Why?* "Why are we doing what we do?" We may make the assumption that all is well, and we are on course. That may not be the case.

One thing the "Why?" question may do is to encourage the senior leadership to identify those things which have changed in the youth culture, and which may call for an honest evaluation of our methodology or message delivery. We should always ask, "Are we relevant to the culture we seek to reach?"

I hope that Young Life will always ask hard questions of itself. This will be a sign of true humility, and will reveal a heartfelt desire to follow God's leading in all of its undertakings. In my next letters I should like to ask the "Why?" questions concerning several programmatic expressions of the mission. Things like club, camping, and Campaigners. Have you ever considered why we do those things? I encourage you to do just that, and maybe some of the things we learned over the years will be helpful to you today.

Why We Do Club

Dear Young Life Leader,

Today I wish to consider with you the "Why?" of the *club*.

The club continues to be the primary vehicle Young Life uses for a regular proclamation of the gospel to kids on the outside. Is it a perfect vehicle? Certainly not. Is it under constant study and experimentation to see how it might be improved? Hopefully, yes.

The mission began with large gatherings of young people, such as the tent meetings I have already described, and also "Mass Meetings," "Rooftop Rallies" at hotels, and high school assemblies. That was the order of the day, and it fit with Jim Rayburn's background, being the son of a Presbyterian evangelist.

Young Life has always wished to be "incarnational" in its approach. This means it has sought to be "present with" and "alongside of" young people. It is relational in its style. This became more difficult to pull off using the circus tent model.

Jim asked my mother and father if there could be a weekly gathering of kids at our home in Dallas. We had a large scout cabin in the back pasture that he wished to use for these meetings.

Young people in those years were a culture which enjoyed gathering together in social groupings. Because of this, Jim and the early leaders hit upon the club idea. Clubs would be open to all kids. They would be lively and fun, informal, friendly, and they would never last more than one hour. The most important time in each meeting would be when the Scriptures were opened, and Jesus was proclaimed in a winsome and powerful manner.

Clubs met on weeknights. Probably the two reasons for this were that high school activities and games often were on weekends, and also that the leaders did not wish to appear competitive with weekend church programs and youth groups.

Jim called that first club meeting at our home "Club 37." He knew that if he had called it "Club #1," we would not have been impressed with the size of his organization. So, dumb us, we came to this thing thinking he, or someone, had at least thirty-six other clubs going somewhere!

This one club was for all the high schools in Dallas, of which there were only six or seven. Jim and the leaders began to do contact work at all those schools. I remember him coming to my school for our athletic practices and games. It was most unusual for anyone to come to our practices because our teams were not very good. But there he was, learning our names and making small talk with players and coaches. We thought it was neat that someone showed up.

The music in club was mostly gospel choruses, hymns, and patriotic war songs. The Second World War was in full force, and some of the boys in that club would soon be in military service. Some of them would sacrifice their lives for our country. (Born in 1929, I was too young to serve.)

In ensuing days, as more clubs came on the scene throughout the country, certain patterns developed. Meetings were held in the homes of kids. The singing was accompanied by a piano.

Kids sat on the floor. Club talks centered on the Person of Jesus Christ as revealed in the Gospels. An invitation to receive Christ always was given. Kids were encouraged to stay after club if they wished to talk about their faith. The whole thing was designed to attract young people who were on the outside of faith. The atmosphere was upbeat, fun, and inclusive for all school groupings.

Today's youth culture has changed radically. Young people have multiple and diverse values, often dictated by computer and internet technology (and who knows what in a few years' time!). Yet I believe the basic premise for the club continues. Look back at how I described my club experience seventy years ago. Are those essential elements in your club? Do all kinds of kids feel welcome? Are they still being presented with the timeless truths of the gospel of Jesus Christ, expressed in terms they understand? Is club a joyful, fun place? Is it a mix of permissive and wholesome?

The times definitely change. We haven't used pianos in clubs for decades, and we stopped singing patriotic war songs when World War II ended. There is no way that I am suggesting a return to those things in order for you to have a successful club. But do ask yourself the question, "How can we make our club attractive to non-Christian kids, and positively proclaim the truth of the gospel in a way that kids will listen?" Your club is going to look different from our "Club 37" in a lot of ways, but in the most important ways, I hope it hasn't changed a bit!

God bless you as you make it happen for those young people to whom you go!

Mitch

Why We Do Camping

Dear Young Life Leader,

Let's look at another "Why?" question: *Why do we do camping with kids?*

Of all the programmatic expressions of Young Life, the camping ministry undoubtedly is the most renowned. Many thousands of young people have made faith commitments while attending a Young Life camp! Probably, there is no other camping organization in the world that has reached so many kids for Christ. Why did the mission hit upon this remarkable vehicle for the proclamation of the gospel, and why is it so effective?

To begin properly, I should relate some history.

In the 1930s, before seminary and Young Life, Jim, an ordained minister, served with the Presbyterian Board of Home Missions. His ministry emphasis even then was with young people who were not in the church.

While serving in New Mexico, Jim discovered that an effective way to reach kids was to take them on camping trips into the mountains. It was a primitive style of camping, but within it was the discovery of timeless principles, which ultimately shaped Young Life's extensive camping ministry.

I believe there are three levels of "contact" by a leader with non-Christian young people. The first is simply "being seen" in places where those kids congregate. The second is to learn their names and enter into conversation with them. The third, and highest level, is when leaders create opportunities to share in some experience with them. Usually it is then when relationships are established. Camping often has provided the setting for this experience of meaningful relationships.

Here is the way it worked for me while I was in high school. One day, Jim persuaded several of us guys in "Club 37" to go with him for a five-day camping trip in the East Texas hills. We got permission from our parents, collected our bedrolls, and piled into his car, and one other vehicle, for the three-hour drive.

You can't believe the place where we ended up! Jim had received permission from a property-owner friend of his to establish our campsite. It was quite remote, and anything but deluxe. We hoped it would not rain, since we had no tents. On this primitive site we were about to experience one of the very first Young Life camps!

During the first night, as we were trying unsuccessfully to get comfortable in our bedrolls on the East Texas rocks, Jim pulled out an air mattress and started blowing it up. We watched when soon he rolled out his blankets and stretched out in relative comfort. Most of us had not seen an air mattress, and certainly, we didn't appreciate the fact that our fearless leader had one, and we did not. What we didn't know was that Jim often had terrible migraine headaches, and that someone had loaned to him the mattress so that he could get some sleep during the camping trip.

Some time, in the middle of the night, while he was asleep, a couple of us crawled quietly over to Jim's mattress and unscrewed the valve. To this day, I can remember the sound of the escaping air, and the feeling of accomplishment we had in this prank. *Sssssssssss* ...

As the mattress deflated, and Jim was lowered upon the rocks, he did not move, nor did he open his eyes. All he said, quietly, was, "Blow it up, boys!"

And we did!

But do you know how hard it is to blow up an air mattress with someone lying on it? We took turns blowing. It sounds crazy, but we might have blown for hours if he had told us to do so. That's how much we thought of this man, who led us to Jesus!

There was not a lot to do in those East Texas hills. The "program" consisted mostly of hunting rattlesnakes and armadillos, and taking a few hikes. Each night after our supper, which Jim prepared, we sat around the campfire. These were special times, when Jim would take out his New Testament and beautifully and powerfully tell us the stories of Jesus. No one I have ever heard could tell those stories as he could! And, of course, there was much laughter sprinkled through it all.

Jim knew that an experience like this could be life-changing. And for me it was. I had to move outside of my usual day-to-day environment, routine, and comfort zone. I was challenged physically and emotionally, and I became more in touch with my personal vulnerability. I discovered that I didn't need my "stuff" at home in order to have a great time. My respect for Jim, and my friendship with him, deepened significantly. I saw him in ways I had not seen him before. I learned more about relating to my peers. I saw God in nature, and in Scripture, and, most of all, in my leader. All of these things made me more receptive to the truth of Jesus!

Now I understand "why" I was invited to go on this camping trip. And really, it's no different for kids today. The same foundational principles apply. Here are the primary reasons why we have done camping for all of these years:

1. At a camp, there are opportunities daily for adventure and new experiences. Often this prepares young people to open their lives to the great adventure of faith.

2. At a camp, kids are free from the distractions of technology, and free from the influence of local peers or family members. They are able to make their own decisions concerning their commitment to Jesus.

3. God speaks through his creation, as revealed in the camp setting.

4. Camps provide a platform for an unbroken proclamation of the gospel story.

5. A cabin leader is in a unique position to influence kids, interpret the talks, and explain how one may have a relationship with Jesus.

6. Work Crew kids and Summer Staff often establish healthy models for kids to follow.

7. The atmosphere of fun and friendship is a wonderful new experience for many. Barriers toward the gospel are broken down and stereotypes of rigid Christianity are changed.

8. In a camp setting young people are able to focus upon the message, and reflect upon its personal meaning. They become aware of a spiritual life within them that needs to be nourished.

9. When program staff and entertainment people are truly funny and creative, kids are appreciative of this, another expression of love.

10. Camping leaves lasting impressions—memories that last a lifetime, along with permanent changes in attitudes and behavior.

For many years we have sought to give all kids an experience like I had with Jim. We provide a camp program that is sensitive to their culture. Camping works for all kids—suburban, urban, small town, international, and kids with disabilities. Here they are introduced to a new relationship with Jesus, with themselves, and with others. We seek to give them the best time of their lives, full of surprises and meaningful relationships. Most of all, we provide an attractive setting for the proclamation of the eternal, life-changing gospel of Jesus! These are reasons why we do camping with young people all over the world!

Today, when I see the fabulous camp properties which God has so graciously given for us to use, I remember how it all started, and my heart sings! How far things have come from those East Texas hills! I celebrate the exponential growth of camping, both in its quantity and in its quality! Only the Lord knows how many young people have and will become followers of Jesus through this wonderful vehicle.

Thanks be to God!

Mitch

Why We Do Campaigners

Dear Young Life Leader,

In this letter I wish to look with you at the question, *Why do we do Campaigners?*

On the surface, the question seems quite simple. But there are theological and practical implications which are important. And there are ecclesiological implications which should not be overlooked by anyone engaged in a mission such as Young Life.

As I have already written you, the name "Campaigners" has its roots in the early tent meetings conducted by Jim Rayburn. These large Christian outreach gatherings with high school kids were called "Young Life Campaigns." Then as various mission programs developed, such as the club, the word "Campaign" was dropped from the organization's corporate name. Today we have simply "Young Life" as our name.

"Campaigners" became the name given to groups of kids focusing upon Christian nurture and discipleship. (I never have liked the name. It doesn't really describe the purpose of the group. We are not asking kids to participate in a "campaign." But the name continues with us today, and that's okay.)

Jesus was about nurture and discipleship with his closest followers. As he travelled with them, taught them, rebuked them, and prayed with them, important things were happening in their lives. Ultimately he committed his life-changing purposes in the world to this small band of people. How confident he was in himself, and in the sustaining and enabling power of the Holy Spirit living within those disciples!

As leaders, we must be committed to encouraging and teaching new believers. The Holy Spirit will enable us to embody Jesus with them. We pray that they will draw ever-closer to him, glorifying the Father and doing his will. Only in their relationship with Jesus will they discover who they are, and only then will they find true meaning for their lives.

God is entrusting you with these wonderful young believers. You are on holy ground! Jesus said, "Feed my sheep." In this endeavor he retains his ownership of the sheep. They are not *your* sheep. We should never become possessive of any kids in our ministries. But we are called to be "good shepherds" for those in our pasture, and to nurture and feed them until they recognize Jesus' voice for themselves.

Why Campaigners? Here are some reasons …

• It is in Campaigners that many young people will begin to understand the life-changing implications of their decision to be a follower of Jesus. Here they will take their baby steps in a walk with Christ.

• They will have their first taste of being in the family of Jesus, and the importance of being in community with others in the faith journey.

• Our prayer is that this will lead to an understanding of the Church worldwide. Young people need to know that the Church is so much larger than Young Life! It is a global community of believers who love and worship Jesus, and who need one another in living out his purposes in the world.

• Kids are bound to have questions about God and their life of faith. They need a safe place to ask anything on their hearts. They need some place to be transparent and open about their fears and doubts.

• Many kids have never read the Bible, nor do they own one. Right from the beginning they need to understand that these things we talk about in clubs and camps are not our ideas. It is in Campaigners that countless numbers of kids have been introduced to the Holy Scriptures that reveal to us the eternal truths of God the Father, God the Son, and God the Holy Spirit.

• The spiritual disciplines of prayer, Scripture reading and memorization, biblical study, and meditation often are begun by kids in Campaigners.

• Campaigner kids may be very helpful to their leaders as they give feedback on how things are going in a club situation, how the message is being received, and what might make things better.

• Corporate prayer should be taught and experienced each week in a Campaigner group. These lessons will last a lifetime. Perhaps the greatest desire for our Campaigner kids is that they will become men and women of prayer!

• Campaigners is intended to help new young believers in their walks with Christ. Young Life is not to become their "church." The Church is made up of all the followers of Jesus throughout the world and embraces every culture and ethnicity.

The Church exists for worship, nurture, and mission. Young Life is only a part of the greater Church, and primarily is the Church in mission. We fail any young person if we teach anything else, either by word or example! It is most important that we define well our identity and our mission. God has called us for a specific task ... to reach young "outsiders" with the good news of Jesus!

May God bless you as you teach others to follow him more closely—

Mitch

Prayers for Your Campaigners

Dear Young Life Leader,

Jesus performed seven miracles which are recorded in the Gospel of John (Jim had a series of club messages on this, "The Seven Signs," that many of us adopted as our own, as I recounted earlier). These remarkable events helped many to believe in Jesus. And they help us today to anticipate the divine power of our Lord. He wishes for us to pray very large prayers. *Nothing is impossible with him.* He still can work miracles.

Here are seven large prayer requests for your Campaigner kids. Please pray these requests often, and expect to see the wonderful ways that God works in their lives. Jesus took a little boy's simple lunch and fed five thousand people with it. And he will bless your new young followers of Jesus as they also give themselves in faith to him each day. Your role with them is to encourage their commitment to Jesus as Lord. Pray—

1. That your Campaigners will grow in their understanding of what it means to be a true follower of Jesus in a world that needs to know him.

2. That the love, grace, and forgiveness of Jesus will be seen in them as they live among their peers and with their families. It is our prayer that moms and dads will notice positive changes in these young people as they begin walking with Jesus.

3. That they will become persons of prayer, learning to live in the presence of God, and depending upon him for everything.

4. That they will learn to read, study, memorize, and pray the Scriptures, embracing them as the Word of God. Hebrews 4:12 says, "For the Word of God is living and active. Sharper than any double-edged sword, it penetrates even to dividing soul and spirit, joints and marrow; it judges the thoughts and attitudes of the heart." Jesus is the Living Word, and he causes the written Word to come alive in us.

5. That they will recognize the call of God upon their lives to serve the poor and needy of the world. In Matthew 25 we read where Jesus said,

> "Then the righteous will answer him, 'Lord, when did we see you hungry and feed you, or thirsty and give you something to drink? When did we see you a stranger and invite you in, or needing clothes and clothe you? When did we see you sick or in prison and go to visit you?'
>
> "The King will reply, 'I tell you the truth, whatever you did for one of the least of these brothers of mine, you did for me.'"

Campaigner kids need to know how closely Jesus identifies with the poor and needy. He is the lowly, humble Christ who stands beside them. When we minister to the poor we actually are ministering to Jesus himself!

6. That they will bring their friends on the outside to Jesus, by whatever means God gives. Jesus' final words to his disciples were, "Go into all the world and make disciples …"(cf. Matthew 28:19). May their motivation for doing this be as Paul revealed in 2 Corinthians 5:14, "For Christ's love compels us …"

7. That they will become active in the church, attending worship, growing and serving in a faith community as God leads. Campaigner kids need to understand that God is alive and powerfully present in the world *beyond* Young Life!

As a leader you are in a most privileged position with young people. Some of them will continue to be lifelong friends of yours. Claudia and I often are in touch with former kids who years before were in one of our Young Life clubs. They are all over the U.S. and the world now, living out a variety of vocations and ministries.

And it is only natural that some of your Campaigner kids later in their journey with Christ will assume staff and leadership responsibilities within the Young Life mission. It worked that way for me, and I won't be surprised if it happens to you, too.

Until next time—

Mitch

Why We Use Humor

Dear Young Life Leader,

One of the most distinctive qualities of Young Life has been its use of humor. Again, this goes back to our founder, Jim Rayburn. His sense of humor was one of his greatest characteristics. In a day when religion for most of us teenagers was not considered a lot of fun, Jim brought this wonderful new dimension into our experience. He helped us to laugh, even as he told Bible stories.

Whether it was recounting an experience, or bringing us into a ridiculous situation, or using an effective play on words, or telling a joke, Jim was masterful. What was so entertaining about him was how tickled he would get at his own humor. We found ourselves laughing at a joke because he seemed to enjoy it so much himself. His laughter was remarkably contagious!

The eminent theologian, Karl Barth, said, "Laughter is the nearest thing to the grace of God." My own experience would bear this out. When I heard Jim speak in that tent, across from Fair Park in Dallas, I knew I had never heard anything like it. Humor was beautifully woven throughout the proclamation of the gospel of grace. Soon each of us would experience this grace in Jesus.

The reason for humor in Young Life is to break down the barriers kids often have toward the gospel, and religion in general. We are not trying to be professional entertainers. We are communicators of the gospel, and if sometimes being ridiculous is helpful in that process we will certainly go that route.

Over the years I have been involved with Young Life entertainment, doing skits, playing my valve trombone, singing in various groups, being program director for several camp properties, and in developing appropriate humor for club talks. I have seen how important it is to plan, prepare, and evaluate any use of humor. In many ways this is an "art form," and it needs to be taken seriously. As you continue your involvement as a leader I would like to give you some encouragement, as well as cautions, concerning humor.

Always keep in mind that the reason for humor in our ministry is *the breaking down of barriers*. Let's be careful not to over-spiritualize all of this. Our entertainment stuff in camp does not need somehow to follow the content of the gospel proclamation. As program directors we don't need to teach anything, except that believers can have fun! Sure, our team often would say a brief prayer together before doing an entertainment night at camp, but the prayer was for this thing to be funny, and enjoyable for the campers. That was all we asked.

Humor in Young Life must always be in good taste. Never do we need to cross over the line into crude or borderline, or bathroom humor, in order to get a laugh.

The most dangerous form of humor is humor at someone else's expense. Anything that puts kids down, or makes fun of them, runs the risk of backfiring. It is most appropriate, however, to make fun of ourselves.

What is performed on television should not be our model. Surely we can come up with better ideas than yelling and scream-ing, hyper-slapstick, or crude forms of entertainment. Being loud is not necessarily being funny, and being repetitious is not necessarily being creative.

The safest and most effective humor usually is "situation humor." This is telling a story in some ridiculous way. The first skit we saw was Jim Rayburn acting out all the parts in the story of "Little Red Riding Hood." He did this one night beside a campfire during one of the first camps in Texas. (The story was enhanced by an unplanned event, when Jim stumbled into the fire—not to be harmed only because of quick action on his part. We thought this was one of the funniest things we had ever seen!)

Music offers great opportunities for humor. Again, we need to come up with excellent, quality stuff. The early leaders drilled that into us! Young Life was formed with a small team of gifted musicians in the Campaigners Quartet, a superb group of Dallas Seminary men, anchored with its premier bass singer, George Sheffer. These guys did high school assemblies, with Jim speak-ing, all over the city of Dallas, and in many larger gatherings of kids in mass meetings and clubs.

The first entertainment team at Star Ranch, in 1946, was made up of fairly competent "note-readers." The "Gut-Bucket Four" (Sarah Rhodes, Orien Johnson, Tom Bade, and yours truly) were musicians, not just noise-makers. Phil McDonald, also a member of the Star Ranch entertainment team, was accomplished on the accordion. And soon, Jim Shelton, legendary pianist-entertainer-program director-camp speaker, arrived at Frontier Ranch. These were some of the early pioneers in Young Life entertainment. Many talented men and women would follow in years thereafter. The honor roll includes Fred and Ann Vagle, Dick Lowey, Reid Carpenter, Jack Carpenter, the Sylte sisters (Deanna, Deanda, and Joan), Fred Langston, Dottie Malouf, Jay Grimstead, Rick Yates, Steff Steinhorst, and Mike Ashburn. On a personal level, I am thankful for the way my own kids were exposed to an abundance of wholesome and creative humor growing up in the Young Life environment. I think particularly of our son Tim—I know his great sense of timing and wit were influenced by countless weeks at camp enjoying great program directors. This served him well when years later he became a church youth pastor.

Humor is an important ingredient of a Young Life talk. This will take practice as you discover the style of humor that fits your personality. It may be a play on words, or telling a joke, or recounting a humorous experience you have had, or creating a hypothetical situation (a "what if?" scenario). Please do not think you must be hilarious in order to be an effective communicator. Be who you are, and use whatever gifts God has given you! Brennan Manning, in one of his books, has a unique quote, "Be who you is, 'cause if you ain't who you is, you is who you ain't."

I'm thankful for you, and your continued ministry with kids. Let's not take ourselves too seriously, even as we take very seriously our calling!

Sincerely in Christ,

Mitch

Why We Have Committees

Dear Young Life Leader,

Today I wish to look with you at the question, *Why do we have committees for local areas?*

For the first ten years of existence as an organization there was just one budget for the entire mission of Young Life. All ministries and staff were supported out of this same entity. Support funds were raised by Jim Rayburn, who contacted a few friends around the country.

If there was not enough money in the account, staff were not paid. Sometimes the staff received short checks, or even zero-dollar checks. (The check actually read "$0.00." I never could figure out why the zero-dollar checks. The volunteer accountant must have thought he needed to do that, or else he had a weird sense of humor.)

There were no local committees—only a small national Board of Directors, which accepted the budget each year and provided most of the funding themselves. At the end of each fiscal year Jim would do his travel and fundraising journey, and we would all pray fervently for the success of his efforts. Without exception, each year, the money always came in, evidencing the gracious hand of God's blessing, and a definite answer to prayer. It also proved Jim to be an excellent fundraiser.

Because there was no local committee sponsoring and endorsing Young Life in an area, staff and leaders could be misunderstood in their purposes, and could be vulnerable to rumors. A typical suspicion, held by some local adults and parents, was that we were Communists!

Area committees were formed, and continue today, for the following purposes and functions:

1. To provide a *partnership* with local staff and leaders, working together on the strategy for reaching kids in the area with the gospel of Jesus Christ.

2. To provide a base of *prayer support* for the ministry.

3. To develop a strategy for *financial support* for the area, authorizing the annual budget, and conducting the annual fund campaign.

4. To ensure the *credibility* of the local Young Life ministry, with parents, school officials, pastors, business and professional leaders, and the community.

5. To partner with staff in *evaluating* the effectiveness of the ministry.

I believe it is safe to say that without a committee in a local area the ministry is in a most vulnerable position!

The role of the staff and leaders with the committee is to inform them on a regular basis of what is going on with kids, tell them actual real-life stories, share prayer requests, invite suggestions concerning how the ministry is being received in the area, and stay in touch concerning finances.

The committee chairman often becomes a best friend of the leader. They share a mutual heartfelt concern for kids who are on the outside!

In 1956 Jim Rayburn sent me to the San Francisco Bay Area with the admonition, "Get out there and get something going!" Claudia and I headed west in our station wagon with our one-year-old son. We had no idea what we were getting into, and deep down I was scared to death.

We found a rather dingy apartment in Berkeley. One night, soon after arriving, I drove up into the Berkeley hills just to see the view of the city at night. It was an awesome experience! I looked across the Bay and there were the lights of four-and-a-half-million people.

I sat in my car and cried.

I wish I could say that I saw them as Jesus did when he wept over the city of Jerusalem, but that would not be honest. Frankly, I was overwhelmed with doubts and fears. All I could do was pray a desperate prayer from my loneliness, "Lord, please give me a friend to do this with!" and I drove back to the apartment.

God answered that prayer in a marvelous way. Days later I met a businessman named Ted. We became great friends, and together we had the privilege of seeing the Bay Area become one of the most remarkable Young Life regions in the country, with committees everywhere, and hundreds of kids coming to faith in the next ten years. A committee chairman became my lifelong friend in ministry. That businessman, Ted Johnson, not only continues to be my close friend to this day, but after he retired from his business career he went on full-time Young Life staff, including a stint as the interim President. In fact, Ted was one of the main folks who encouraged me to write these letters to you.

It may not happen just that way with you, but I can assure you that one of your greatest gifts from God will be your committee!

God bless you.

Mitch

Why Are You a Young Life Leader?

Dear Leader,

Please deal today with the very basic question, *Why are you a Young Life leader?* In other words, what motivates you to reach out to kids? Most likely you will answer with more than one reason, such as:

—I see a great need among young people today who don't know Jesus.

—Adolescence is such an important time for life-impacting decisions.

—I believe Young Life is on the right track in its relational and Christ-centered approach to evangelism with young people.

—I came to faith in Young Life and I want to be a part of whatever it does.

—There are few organizations which have been so effective in outreach to non-Christian adolescents.

—I like the "feel" of this mission, its style of ministry, and its sense of humor.

—Some of my best friends are in Young Life, and it is good to stay connected.

—A Young Life camp may be the most effective vehicle for leading kids to Jesus. I want to be a part of something so effective.

—I think I have some gifts and abilities which may be useful. I hope so.

—I like the way Young Life keeps up with the adolescent culture and adapts its approach and message to where kids are today.

—Young Life is biblical in its method and message.

—Young Life obviously is blessed by God in its amazing growth in the United States and the world. It is exciting to be a part of something that definitely is making a difference.

—I love the emphasis upon reaching all kids—every culture and background, urban, suburban, small town, college, kids with disabilities, international, teen moms, etc.

Each of the above reasons for being a leader is valid and important. No doubt you will respond wholeheartedly and thankfully to many of them in future days.

In this letter I wish to consider with you what I believe to be the most important "reason why" for doing Young Life. (I do not include it in the above list.) Let's look at one of the post-resurrection appearances of Jesus, described in John 21:1–17. Hear the Word of the Lord:

> Afterward Jesus appeared again to his disciples, by the Sea of Galilee. And it happened this way: Simon Peter, Thomas (called Didymus), Nathaniel from Cana in Galilee, the sons of Zebedee, and two other disciples were together. "I'm going out to fish," Simon Peter told them, and they said, "We'll go with you." So they went out and got into the boat, but that night they caught nothing.
>
> Early in the morning, Jesus stood on the shore, but the disciples did not realize that it was Jesus.
>
> He called out to them, "Friends, haven't you any fish?"
>
> "No," they answered.
>
> He said, "Throw your net on the right side of the boat and you will find some." When they did, they were unable to haul the net in because of the large number of fish.
>
> Then the disciple whom Jesus loved said to Peter, "It is the Lord!" As soon as Simon Peter heard him say, "It is the Lord," he wrapped his outer garment around him (for he had taken it off) and jumped into the water. The other disciples followed in the boat, towing the net full of fish, for they were not far from shore, about a hundred yards. When they landed, they saw a fire of burning coals there with fish on it, and some bread.

Jesus said to them, "Bring some of the fish you have just caught."

Simon Peter climbed aboard and dragged the net ashore. It was full of large fish, 153, but even with so many the net was not torn. Jesus said to them, "Come and have breakfast." None of the disciples dared ask him, "Who are you?" They knew it was the Lord. Jesus came, took the bread and gave it to them, and did the same with the fish. This was now the third time Jesus appeared to his disciples after he was raised from the dead.

When they had finished eating, Jesus said to Simon Peter, "Simon son of John, do you truly love me more than these?"

"Yes, Lord," he said, "you know that I love you."

Jesus said, "Feed my lambs."

Again Jesus said, "Simon son of John, do you truly love me?"

He answered, "Yes, Lord, you know that I love you."

Jesus said, "Take care of my sheep."

The third time he said to him, "Simon son of John, do you love me?"

Peter was hurt because Jesus asked him the third time, "Do you love me?" He said, "Lord, you know all things; you know that I love you."

Jesus said, "Feed my sheep."

As we walk through this story, please "be there." Bring all of your senses, your imagination, your feelings, your intuition, along with your reason and logic. Prayerfully bring all that you can of yourself to this text. This truly is the way we should read all of Scripture. And always we must ask the Holy Spirit to guide us in our journey.

It is only a few days now after the crucifixion and burial of Jesus. Seven of the disciples are together. Peter is one of them. Certainly he must be feeling a lot of pain and guilt over his three-fold public denial of Jesus during the so-called trial of the Lord. He blurts out, "I'm going fishing!"

Peter most likely feels a deep need to succeed at *something*. He has failed miserably as a disciple. "At least," he thinks, "I still can fish!" He may not be a good disciple, but he has made his living on this Sea of Galilee. He wishes to return to something familiar, something he can handle.

"We'll go with you!" the other disciples reply. This is a beautiful response to their friend. Some of these guys are not fishermen, yet they do not want to see Peter go it alone. He is not in good shape mentally and emotionally. They feel a need to stay close to him. Each of us should be sensitive to hurting people in our lives. They should not be left alone. These friends may need a phone call, e-mail, or visit from us today.

After loading the net into the boat, out they go for their fishing expedition. Peter guides them to the place where the fish usually school at this time of day. Their first pass nets nothing. This lack of success continues in subsequent passes, even after changing locations several times. Hours pass and the men are growing silent. They can only imagine what Peter is feeling ... "It is hopeless! Now I can't even fish!"

All night long they continue to fish, with no catch. Time and again they bring in an empty net. Finally these weary men give up and head for shore. The morning sun is beginning to light the horizon. It is not a happy group of disciples, singing "Row, Row, Row Your Boat" as they come in. Some of them glance quietly at Peter. How is he doing as now he faces another failure?

Nearing the shore they see someone standing on the beach waiting for them. There is not enough light to make out his identity. As they draw closer, this stranger calls out to them, asking the worst question that fishermen can hear if they have been skunked. "Have you caught anything, lads?" (The diminutive word translated in J. B. Phillips' version, "lads," doesn't help their self-esteem one bit! It is like he might be saying, "Have you caught anything, little boys?")

They answer, "No." At least that is what the Scripture reports them saying. They may have said a few more words which were a lot stronger, and which were sensitively filtered out by the Holy Spirit as not edifying.

And then, the stranger has the audacity to say, "Throw the net on the right side of the boat . . ." By now they are approaching the shore. It is too close in for fishing. The net probably will get tangled among rocks and snags. But there is something strangely unusual and familiar about this man on the shore . . . for whatever reasons they throw out the net once again. This time there are fish, so many they are unable to bring in the net.

Then "the disciple whom Jesus loved" said to Peter, "It is the Lord!" That disciple is John, who is the author of this narrative. This sensitive man is the first to recognize Jesus. Don't you love John? I too like to think of myself as the one whom Jesus loves! Don't you?

The first to recognize Jesus is the beloved apostle John. Love always sharpens our vision. We see all things differently when we look through eyes of love. We see the world as God sees it, with all of its hurt and brokenness. When we see kids who don't know Jesus through the eyes of his love they always will look different to us. And probably we will find them hard to get out of our minds.

Upon hearing John's words, Peter puts his cloak back on and jumps into the water to swim to shore. What is that all about? It makes no sense! The boat can get there just as fast, or faster, than he can, swimming. And besides, don't people usually take off their clothes when they go swimming? But love is not always logical, is it? At times people do unusual and illogical things, prompted by love. There is no need to try to figure this out. Peter just wants to be near Jesus! May this always be our heart's desire as well!

The story continues, when Peter and the disciples reach the shore they find Jesus has a fire going with fish on it, and some bread. Jesus says, "Come and have your breakfast." Where did Jesus get the fish and bread? Who knows? He is the creator and sustainer of the universe. But isn't it wonderful that the first thing he does for those exhausted and hungry fishermen is to meet their physical needs! We learn something very important about ministry here. When we go to all kinds of kids, we must remember that some of them will be struggling with heavy-duty problems. There may be addictions, guilt, loneliness, fear, discouragement—the list goes on. In order for us to reach them with the gospel we may need to deal with their personal needs first. Just preaching "Jesus saves!," may not cut it with them.

Jesus has so much he wishes to say to those disciples, but they can't hear him right now. They are too tired and hungry and frustrated. And so he offers them breakfast! Isn't that great?

For centuries the Church has been called to proclaim the gospel of Jesus. But our Lord by example is teaching that we also must confront physical human needs. This will be social action that incarnates the love of Christ. In our John 21 story we hear Jesus say, "If you love me, feed my sheep!" I remember one of our urban brothers sharing with us how hard it is to reach a kid who has a captivating and expensive heroin habit. Often this one can't even hear the gospel until certain things are dealt with. It's all a part of leadership.

The meal is over and the men sit quietly around the fire. Perhaps they feel they are sharing Holy Communion. Jesus once again is offering the elements as he did in the upper room not long before this.

Now it is time to deal with a hurting man, Peter. Jesus has great hopes for this disciple, and his loving heart goes out to him. Three times he asks Peter the very same question, "Simon, do you love me?" In these times he does not use the name "Peter." Peter means "rock." The man is not very rock-like at the moment. So he calls him by his given name, Simon.

Three times we hear Peter's unequivocal response, "Yes, Lord, I love you." We sense he really means this.

The other disciples are listening to every word. What must they be feeling as they hear the painful dialogue, with the same question repeated to their friend three times? Is Jesus being cruel to Peter, working him over like this in the presence of his friends? Far from it!

What we are seeing is the wonderful grace of Jesus. Here is a disciple who has publicly denied him three times. But now Jesus graciously offers to him an opportunity to offset his failure. Three times he is given the chance publicly to confess his faith and love for his Lord! How gracious of Jesus! In this moment I believe Peter is transformed. He will never turn back in his apostolic ministry!

Do you see here the motivation for doing ministry—our "reason why"? Let us not miss it! *We go to kids because God so loved the world that he gave his only son. Through his sacrifice on the cross he loves and forgives the entire world!* All persons need to hear this good news, and be given the opportunity, like Peter, to choose to follow Jesus as his disciple! Second Corinthians 5:14 summarizes: "For Christ's love compels us!" As leaders, then, we are motivated by his love for us and our love for him!

Jesus now admonishes Peter to "Feed my sheep." In this command there is such grace! It implies that Jesus still trusts Peter, in spite of his failure. He invites Peter to nurture and care for his followers!

Sheep are mentioned often in the Bible. Various shepherds play a prominent role in both the Old and New Testaments. Jesus is called the "Lamb of God, who takes away the sin of the world." And he refers to himself as the Good Shepherd. Over and over we hear biblical references to sheep.

When I was in junior high school in Texas my older brother and I raised sheep. We also had pecan trees on our land, so we formed a little business called the Mitchell Brothers Sheep and Nut Company. Sheep are a lot of trouble. Often they wander off and get into some sort of predicament. Our sheep occasionally would get stuck behind the electric fence or fall into the pond, which to us seemed a bit stupid!

Sheep are defenseless and dependent. These wooly creatures look better from a distance than they do close up. Mostly they are followers rather than leaders. They tend to be noisy and at times downright obnoxious. About all they can do well is eat. But sometimes they are irresistibly lovable. Doesn't all of that describe many of the kids you are working with? (Just for fun, go back over that list of characteristics of sheep and make your comparisons.)

Jesus talks about "my sheep." The kids we work with are his. They have been bought with a huge price, on Calvary! They are not our sheep. As shepherd-leaders we are entrusted with their care and feeding.

Please pray with the following questions, and journal your answers. If possible, discuss them with other leaders:

- Taking the Scripture personally will mean answering the same question Jesus asked Peter beside that fire, "Do you love me?" Please hear the question each day of your life, and in some way pray your answer, "Yes, Lord, I love you!"

- How might your love for Jesus be expressed in real-life ways—your mind, emotions, words, actions?

- In order to deepen your love and friendship with Jesus what needs to change in your attitude or behavior?

- Who are the sheep Jesus is asking you to care for? Identify by names and/or groups.

- What will it mean for you to feed and care for the sheep? What actions will you need to take? What changes do you anticipate making?

God bless you as you seek to be a good shepherd!

Mitch

ʃection Three

— Values —

Goldbrick

It was a very exciting day in 1951 when "Round-up Lodge for Boys" became a Young Life camp! This remarkable property in Buena Vista, Colorado, situated at 9,000 feet in elevation on the slopes of Mt. Princeton, was a dream come true. For many years Jim Rayburn had been aware of the camp's existence, but did not imagine that such a place would one day be one of the most significant expressions of the gospel to young people in all the world!

But it happened! Through a series of God-inspired events, Round-up Lodge became Frontier Ranch! An exciting chapter for Young Life was being written, and thousands of young people would hear about Jesus in that unbelievably beautiful setting. Today I don't want to talk about camping, though. Instead I want to tell you a story about a wonderful couple who came on staff when we purchased Frontier and who changed Young Life forever. It will serve as an introduction to a series of letters about values Young Life has long held close.

Until 1951 Young Life was an organization that worked with white, suburban, middle- or upper-class, able-bodied, American high school young people. The first persons of color to join the staff were an African-American couple from Philadelphia named Andrew and Gerry Delaney. They were hired to be the chefs for the newly acquired Frontier Ranch. In ensuing years

"Goldbrick," as Andrew was called, and Gerry would influence Work Crew kids and campers like few others in our mission's history. They were legends!

The previous year, 1950, Jim invited me to join the staff, move to Colorado Springs, and to develop the local Young Life ministry with kids. By that time I had completed my college degree and a year of graduate biblical studies. Also while in college as a volunteer leader I had spent several summers at Star Ranch, Young Life's first camp, in Colorado Springs. I loved that place. But most of all, I loved the Young Life mission. The decision to join the staff was an easy one.

Being single, I moved into a tiny, very rustic log cabin at Star Ranch. When they came on staff in 1951, Goldbrick and Gerry also lived on the property during the school year, as did the Rayburn family. For four years we shared life together in a community of laughter and spiritual growth. Especially did I enjoy the evening dinners prepared by Goldbrick and Gerry! Often during those times Jim would hold forth with his wonderful stories, and the Rayburn kids, whom I drove to school each day, would talk about their day at school, or whatever.

The ministry of Young Life at Colorado Springs High School (now Palmer High) took off. Hundreds of kids were coming to club. Goldbrick and I worked side-by-side, along with a team of volunteer leaders, making contact with as many young people as we could. In that process Goldbrick and I became devoted friends.

It was with Goldbrick and Gerry that I learned what it meant to be a person of color. In many ways I had no clue about the realities of racism in the United States, even though I had grown up in Dallas with its WHITE and COLORED signs segregating all public drinking fountains and restrooms. With these two beautiful people, I "went to school" in the subject.

I remember a day in late December 1951. The snow had covered Star Ranch and all of Cheyenne Mountain with a beautiful white blanket. That evening I went down to the main kitchen and found Goldbrick and Gerry getting ready for their long drive to Philadelphia where they would spend Christmas with family. The kitchen smelled great, as Andy was frying up four chickens.

I asked him what all the chicken was for. He said it was for Gerry and him to eat during their nonstop drive to Philadelphia. "You mean you're not going to stop for meals, or to sleep somewhere for those nights?" I asked.

"Mitch," he answered quietly, "there are no places for us to stop, except to buy gas and a few groceries." I was so naïve! I had forgotten that in many states restaurants and motels were not open to black people. I remember going up the mountain to my cabin and crying as I fell asleep.

One of Young Life's most important historic values is its commitment to urban and multicultural ministries. It did not come about easily. When the camps became integrated, and when we appointed black people to staff leadership positions, some entire committees in the South pulled out, wanting nothing to do with Young Life any longer. We had to close those areas. These were traumatic times in our nation, and in our mission.

But, thank God, things began to change in Young Life. During the tenure of Bill Starr, who succeeded Jim as President, and through the influence of a remarkable band of urban and international staff, Young life headed in the necessary direction for becoming multicultural and multiracial. We are standing on the shoulders of some passionate and gifted leaders!

I pray that Young Life will be relentless in its commitment to reaching young people of all cultures, backgrounds, and personal human conditions, in the United States, and in the world! Jesus will have it no other way! In the Gospel of Matthew we hear him say clearly, "Go and make disciples of *all* people" (cf. Matthew 28:19).

What follows in this section are some thoughts about values—important elements of Young Life's ministry that I pray we never lose.

Excellence

Dear Leader,

We begin now to look at some of the historic values of the mission. These values are the reason why Young Life has been so effective down through the years.

Among all the values there is one that I put at the top of the list. This particular value impacts everything throughout the mission. I am speaking of our radical commitment to *excellence*.

Whether we are talking about the effectiveness of its leaders, the execution of its ministry and programs, the quality of its camp properties, or a long list of other characteristics, there has always been a commitment to excellence in Young Life.

Years ago I read a great quote: "God has not promised us smooth sailing, but he has promised arrival in excellent condition." This is right in line with our experience of Jesus, and what we are thinking about concerning "excellence" in Young Life.

This emphasis has important biblical roots. Jesus came to give people the abundant life, not a "so-so existence." John 10:10 says, "I have come that they may have life, and have it to the full." What could be more meaningful than walking each day in an intimate relationship with Jesus? This defines excellence in living!

As you recall, the first message I heard Jim give in the tent was about Jesus attending a wedding in Cana, when they ran out of wine during the big celebration. Jesus observed some foot-washing water in stone pots standing nearby. That ordinary water he turned into wine. But it was not just your average wine he created. It was absolutely the best! The presiding elder of the feast exclaimed about its superb quality. This first recorded miracle of Jesus in the Gospel of John leads us early on to see that this person, Jesus, is going to personify excellence in all that he says and does!

We have a fabulous message to proclaim! It is the message of the Incarnation. God became a human being, in his son, to redeem our sinful world. We must be excellent in the proclamation of this message! *Never should a leader stand before kids to give a club talk that is ill-prepared, shallow, irrelevant, or unbiblical! The message of the incarnation of God in Jesus Christ absolutely demands excellence in preparation and delivery!*

I believe that every function of the mission calls for excellence. Certainly this includes our contact ministry. The ultimate goal for going where kids are, and for getting to know them and their culture, is to build friendship and trust. If this is done properly, kids will sense the unconditional nature of our friendship with them. They will feel that we are not coming to them to pressure them into a decision or to promote our cause. We are demonstrating unconditional love, which may be defined as, "love for the sake of the person being loved." Excellence in our contact ministry will produce trust.

I have seen some leaders who exude excellence in their contact ministries. They remember names very well. They are good listeners. They put kids at ease in their presence. They understand the culture of those to whom they go. They embody friendship and a joyful spirit. And most of all they seem to be someone who can be trusted.

Camping is another of the important examples of excellence in Young Life. Right from the beginning a standard was set for excellence for each property. Not only must they be physically attractive and unique, but the program must be of top quality and be appealing to young people who are not yet followers of Jesus.

Property ownership for Young Life began with the acquisition of Star Ranch in 1946. Situated on the slopes of Cheyenne Mountain, close to Colorado Springs, this forty-eight-acre property was an absolute gem! I was a teenager on the first Work Crew. Jim instilled in us excellence in the Star Ranch camp property and all of its programs. He was passionate about it. We lived in that atmosphere, which thankfully continues decades later in the current mission of Young Life.

As I look back upon over seventy years that I have been involved with Young Life I am thankful for friendships which continue to this day. And I am grateful for life-changing lessons learned along the way. I have seen how God has enabled the mission to be what it is today. The commitment to excellence is woven into our history.

The quality of staff and leaders, the training they receive, the power in our proclamation of the gospel, our work with Campaigners, the ministry with committees, the way we relate to the church and the community, our approach to hard-to-reach kids, our fundraising and organizational practices, our inter-personal relationships, and most of all, our personal walk with Jesus—may there be excellence in these and all other endeavors as we go forward.

The excellence of our ministry will be determined largely by the depth of our commitment to prayer and intimacy with Jesus—staying near him each day of our lives! Where are you staying these days?

You are part of something having eternal significance. May God bless you and encourage you as you serve him—with excellence!

Mitch

∫ervant Leadership

Dear Leader,

Over the years I have known many gifted leaders who have been effective in their ministry with kids, and in developing other leaders. There seems to be an essential quality in each of them.

A list of desirable leadership qualities might include such things as enthusiasm, promotional and fundraising abilities, the ability to produce good numbers and ministry statistics, and strong management capabilities. These are important abilities but I would not put any of them at the top of the list.

Let's look at Philippians 2:5-8: "Your attitude should be the same as that of Christ Jesus: Who, being in very nature God, did not consider equality with God something to be grasped, but made himself nothing, taking the very nature of a servant, being made in human likeness. And being found in appearance as a man, he humbled himself and became obedient to death—even death on a cross!"

He *humbled* himself! Humility is the hallmark of his life. And it should be for us, and for any truly authentic Christian leader.

The mind, or attitude, of Christ is the "lowly mind." Such a mind would not wish to exert organizational power or control over others. Nor would it crave accolades from others. It is all about treating people with the love of Jesus. First Corinthians 13:4 states, "This love of which I speak is slow to lose patience— it looks for a way of being constructive. It is not possessive: it is neither anxious to impress nor does it cherish inflated ideas of its own importance" (J. B.Phillips translation). What a great description of humility! Here is the basis for "servant leadership," which I believe is the highest and most effective style of leadership for any mission or organization.

There is an important story of Jesus that brings this alive. We find it in John 13:1–17. Jesus is having his last meal with the disciples just hours before his death on the cross. We know it as the Lord's Supper. It is a most holy moment in Christian history, and has been a foundational text for the Church throughout the world.

It is Thursday night. Occasions like this are special for the disciples, but this night seems strangely different from all others.

They share bread and wine, and they sing hymns and psalms. Isn't it encouraging to know that such worship was a part of the disciples' spiritual experience? We don't usually think of Jesus and his disciples as singing together. But this makes it all the more meaningful for us as we sing in our worship times. Prayers, Scripture reading, and singing are so much a part of who we are in the Church. Some of my most unforgettable memories as a young leader are when the staff and leaders would get together and sing. It was an awesome experience of worship as we joined to sing from our hearts such hymns as, "Hallelujah! What A

Savior!," "Fairest Lord Jesus," and "He Arose!" Was this a fore-taste of heaven for us? Yes, I believe it was!

Now Jesus does something that makes some of his friends very uncomfortable. He assumes the role of a servant, taking a towel and basin, and kneeling before each of them to wash their feet. How amazing! The creator and sustainer of the universe is kneeling before ordinary human beings! This is the ultimate personification of servant leadership. Here we see the wonder of the Incarnation!

All of the disciples came into that upper room with dirty feet, but not one of them takes the initiative to be a servant. Something needs to get done, but no one steps forward. Only Jesus, the eternal Son of God, is willing to wash feet!

When it is Peter's turn to have his feet washed he can't handle it. There is no way he will allow Jesus to kneel before him, appearing to beg for his love. Impulsively he rebukes the Lord and commands him not to perform this act. "You will never wash my feet!" says Peter. Is this an evidence of his humility? Probably not. It may more be a sign of his ego, or false humility. As a self-sufficient male, Peter finds it very hard to be in a "receiving posture." It makes him appear vulnerable, or out of control. For some of us, too, it may be hard to admit that we have needs—in fact, that we have dirty feet! As we grow older it seems to get a little easier. I suppose we know ourselves better, and we don't need to keep up an impressive image of sufficiency.

Peter is on very precarious ground when he "commands" Jesus. One must never do that! Yes, God is love … but let us remember, he will always be God! It is not our role to tell God what to do.

Jesus now makes his startling disclosure that one of them will betray him. Each disciple asks, "Is it I, Lord?" Evidently each of them is beginning to realize he has the potential for betrayal. There is a developing sense of honesty among them. I believe it happens this way for those who are followers of Christ. A journey to God often is a journey into oneself, as painful as it may be!

When Jesus has finished washing their feet he puts on his clothes and returns to his place. There is silence. Then he says, "Do you know what I have done for you? Now that I your Lord and teacher have washed your feet, you also should wash one another's feet." It is quite straightforward, isn't it? This is our model for servant leadership.

Henri Nouwen writes about a "bent-over God." This is a God who invites us also to bend over, and in humility to serve one another.

How might humility, or servant-leadership, be expressed through staff and leaders? Here are some of the ways it might occur as we put others ahead of ourselves:

—When all that we do flows out of an intimacy with Jesus in prayer.

—When a leader encourages another leader, or staff person, who is struggling.

—When we pray for each other, and stay in touch.

—When we take a bunch of kids to camp even though they can't pay for it.

—When we ourselves model healthy relationships by serving our families.

—When our ministry area exhibits racial and gender diversity in its leadership and ministry.

—When staff people affirm volunteer leaders just for "hanging in there."

—When we go out of our way for a hard-to-reach kid.

—When we remember someone's name.

—When we call or visit local pastors, priests, or church leaders to keep them informed, to answer questions, and to listen to their concerns.

—When we do those same things with parents.

—When we clean the bus so the driver doesn't have to.

—When people in leadership positions truly listen, seeking to understand those whom they lead.

—When a leader or staff person says, "I'm sorry."

—When we forgive easily.

—When we refuse to make critical judgments about another's motivation.

—When we correct one another in a loving manner.

—When we seek to affirm one another.

—When regularly we thank donors for their support.

—When we leaders share a worldview which is inspired by Jesus.

—When we help the Work Crew clear the tables or take over the dishwashing duties for the night at camp.

—When we listen to Jesus in Scripture, in prayer, in one another, and in the events of our lives, in order to discover God's will for us each day.

—When we work with kids who have physical or emotional disabilities, or with teen moms, or in economically disadvantaged urban situations, all of which require dealing with their physical and emotional needs as well as their spiritual needs.

—When we refuse to take ourselves too seriously, keeping a healthy sense of humor.

The list goes on. There is no telling where this journey will take us as we put others ahead of ourselves the way Jesus did!

God bless you,

Mitch

Young Life and the Church

Dear Leader,

Today I wish to share my heart with you about a most important subject, Young Life and its relationship with the Church. This matter, perhaps too often overlooked, calls for honesty and humility on our part. The Lord's design for his mission in the world certainly includes but goes far beyond the Young Life program. I pray that God will protect us from any appearance of being an independent, totally self-sufficient, and very large organization, out there successfully doing our own thing. Rather, in humility may we join our hearts truly with all followers of Jesus worldwide as we fulfill our particular calling to proclaim the wondrous gospel to kids outside the faith.

In my letter to you discussing the reasons why we have the Campaigners program, I wrote, "Campaigners is intended to help new young believers in their walks with Christ. Young Life is not to become their 'church.' The Church is made up of all the followers of Jesus throughout the world." Young Life is only a part of the larger Church. Specifically, it is the Church in mission. God has called us to reach young people who have not heard or responded to the good news of Jesus.

Jesus' final words to his disciples commissioned them to go and make disciples throughout the world. This has always been the passion of Young Life in its ministry with young people. Why, then, has this mission been misunderstood, and in some situations even resented and seen as competitive with the church?

Ironically, one reason is its success. Over the years Young Life has been privileged to focus upon one specific task—adolescent evangelism. In doing this, the program has been personal, incarnational, and full of fun for all kids. Its extensive camping program especially has had remarkable success, and probably is the largest of its kind in the world today.

Local churches have the same wish to reach young people. Our daughter, Tammy, is an ordained Presbyterian (USA) minister. She and her husband, Tom, are pastors together for the Trinity Presbyterian Church in Anchorage, Alaska. Tammy, of course, grew up in Young Life. She spent many summers with us at some camp property, was a club and Campaigner kid, was on several Work Crews, and was a volunteer leader in college before she attended seminary. All of this gives her a unique perspective on the subject of Young Life and the church. She wrote me recently with some of her reflections:

"In my experience, local churches do try to offer a healthy youth ministry of some kind. They may feel the pain of their own kids losing interest in 'church' and Christianity. They pray that some day their kids will 'come back to church.' They know that adolescents need a specialized ministry. They are acutely aware that the culture today is even 'anti-church.' Every church I have served, regardless of its size, has been very conscious of the need to reach kids. Those which are able put resources and personnel toward building a strong youth ministry. Perhaps many churches do lack a vision for the 'unreached' kid. They tend to focus more on the youth who come to their church."

I believe Tammy has summarized very well the realities we are considering in this letter. It is important to remember that Young Life exists for the primary purpose of reaching the "unchurched"! If we ever lose that focus I am afraid it will no longer be Young Life.

When I left the Young Life staff to become, in ensuing years, the interim pastor for several Presbyterian churches, I learned how it feels to be a minister in a local church, with all of its expectations and demands. But also I saw how it is possible to follow the same principles in church youth programs as in Young Life. I witnessed some programs which were effective in outreach. Each of these had a relational leadership style, a personal and loving touch through committed and gifted leaders, the wonder and power of biblical proclamation, and leaders who kept a sense of humor and adventure in their ministries. These church youth leaders, like Young Life leaders, spent many hours entering the youth culture, and getting to know young people individually, all with a clear focus upon Jesus Christ. It was gratifying to see that the so-called Young Life methodology can be effective in a church setting, even though it may be more difficult for a variety of reasons. Simply put, it is all about biblical, relational, Christ-centered evangelism. Theologically, it may be understood as "incarnational witness."

Do we understand that Young Life is effective not only because of gifted leadership and programmatic capabilities, but because it reflects the essence of what the church is called to be and to do—to be an instrument of God's mission in a needy world? Young Life is part of the Church, the grand fellowship of believers, who are living out the Great Commission in the adolescent world.

In the early days of Young Life, Jim Rayburn, himself an ordained Presbyterian minister, was openly critical of the church for its ineffectiveness in reaching young people outside the church. He gave scorching public criticisms which certainly did not sit well with church leadership. One of his memorable statements was, "Bringing our kids into the church is like putting live chicks under a dead hen."

So, really, it is no surprise that there was a great deal of opposition from pastors and church leaders. In fact, in the early 1950s most major denominations published national documents criticizing Young Life, and asking church members not to participate in its programs. These were difficult days in our relationship with the larger body of Christ.

Even though national statistics revealed much validity in Jim's criticisms, Young Life did not find itself in the favor of many churches. It was viewed as a competitive, independent organization. It didn't help that many young people were excited about Young Life and substituted it for their church.

Bill Starr, who followed Jim as Young Life's President, joined with other key leaders of the organization in asserting that Young Life must revise its understanding and practices toward the institutional church. Staff and leaders were asked to view themselves as part of the larger Church, and to relate in dialogue and cooperation with local Protestant and Catholic churches.

A Church Relations Advisory Committee, made up of leading pastors and priests across the nation, was formed to meet regularly and to advise and enter into mutual dialogue with the senior leaders of Young Life concerning theological and church issues. This afforded some important changes in Young Life and in its relationship with the church.

In 1963, Dr. Emile Cailliet, a renowned biblical scholar, theologian, and professor at Princeton Theological Seminary, wrote a book on Young Life. It was scholarly and theologically astute. Dr. Cailliet had been invited by Jim to attend a week of camp at Frontier Ranch as an adult guest. I happened to be the camp director for most of that summer, and I shall not forget the feelings I had as a young leader each night giving biblical talks about Jesus to kids, with that brilliant man in the audience! But he could not have been more supportive. We became good friends. Later he wrote in his book the following words concerning Young Life and the Church.

> There is no question that Young Life is a genuine expression of the Christian mission and thus of the Church. Freely granting that an expression is not an equivalent, it is only fair to acknowledge the Christian witness and achievement of Young Life as that of a genuinely Christian movement. As to its Church connections, Young Life is definitely nonsectarian. It has a definite ministry to see that no young person misses his appointed right to encounter a positive Christian witness and decide for himself whether or not to acknowledge the claims of Jesus Christ for his

life. This task is so staggering in scope, and the need for it among our teenagers so great, that Young Life chooses to leave involved doctrinal matters to the various churches, while concentrating its attention on the centrality of Christ in the Gospel. (*Young Life*, Emile Cailliet, Harper and Row, p. 53.)

I encourage you as a Young Life leader to hold a biblical view of the Church, and to celebrate the variety of ways the Church in the world is being used to proclaim the Good News of Jesus. We must educate ourselves as to how the Church is ministering within a variety of cultures and religions. It faces great challenges, experiencing hardships and persecution as it seeks to honor the Great Commission of Jesus.

Certainly the Church has its flaws. After all, it is made up of human beings like us, stuck in our own views and ways of thinking! But the Church is the body of Christ, the visible expression of the redemptive community of Jesus. We all are part of that expression, so let us prayerfully consider our role as church members and committed participants in the mission of the Church.

As the years go on, may you be privileged, as I have been, to see kids you have known take their places in the Church of Jesus Christ. There is nothing more fulfilling! My heart sings when I see kids who may have been quite distant from the faith grow in their relationships with Jesus, establishing Christian homes, studying the Scriptures, and becoming active in their churches. I run into them all over the world. Some are serving as pastors and youth leaders. Some are Young Life staff or volunteer leaders.

Some are missionaries or Christian workers in the U.S. or in distant lands. I love it! It makes it all worth it!

Here are a few questions, prayerfully to consider:

- Are you an active member of a local church, and are you modeling for kids a commitment to the church's ministry?

- Do the young people in your club and Campaigners learn from you that as believers they are part of the larger Church of Jesus Christ in the world, and as such need to be involved in regular worship and mission in his Church?

- As a leader, do you make contact with local ministers, priests, and youth leaders, keeping them informed, expressing a spirit of cooperation and dialogue?

May you know that your Young Life ministry is leading young people to an understanding and experience of the breadth and depth of Christ's Church worldwide.

And today may we listen with the ears of our hearts to the timeless final words of Jesus to his disciples, recorded in Matthew 28:16–18, "All authority in heaven and on earth has been given to me. Therefore go and make disciples of all nations, baptizing them in the name of the Father and of the Son and of the Holy Spirit, and teaching them to obey everything I have commanded you." This is the great mission of the Church in the world, given to us by Jesus. I am so thankful that Young Life is a wonderful part of that mission!

God bless you!

Mitch

Understanding the Youth Culture

Dear Leader,

Let's talk about the youth culture. What are teenagers like today? There was a time when I felt I knew adolescents pretty well. I was comfortable around them and able to communicate on their level. Now I recognize that those days probably are over. Much of their world is foreign to me. Their technological capabilities, communication style, music, and vocabulary often are areas of mystery. I do not grieve the loss, nor do I make some ridiculous attempt to "get back into the game." Nope ... this is where *you* come in as a Young Life leader!

I know there are certain principles for youth ministry which are timeless, such as remembering kids' names. But there are areas of the youth culture today that require leaders to be devoted students of that culture. I am writing to encourage you to be just that. Furthermore, you may be called upon to work in a cross-cultural or international setting, or with kids who have physical or mental disabilities. That may make it even more challenging.

A very important principle for youth leaders may be described as "going where kids are." This means not only establishing geographical proximity with them, but also will result in cultural and personal nearness. Perhaps the greatest compliment you as a leader will ever hear from a young person, expressed verbally or non-verbally, is "You are my friend!" It will make your day!

A good leader of young people does not try to "be one of the kids." I have seen leaders attempt this and fall flat—not a pretty sight! Let's face it, we no longer are one of them. And really, they do not wish for us to try to be. We enter their world as a loving person who understands where they are, and can tune into their feelings.

Volumes have been written about the adolescent culture. Seminars have been given, and studies made. I'll not try to duplicate any of them, but rather to make an appeal to you as a leader. Please, do everything in your power to become a good student of today's youth culture!

Are there some common themes, or desires, which describe young people today? I believe so. Many years ago a sociologist named W. I. Thomas proposed his Four Wishes, a summary list of the things most important to all humans, including adolescents. The "wishes" are: *recognition, response, security*, and *the new experience*.

Isn't it true that all young people have a basic desire to be a person who matters? Over the years some of the loneliest young people I have known have been those who did not feel they were of much value. They were nobody, just a small blur on the landscape of the adolescent world. Here is the reason why we work so hard to learn the names of kids. It is one very important way to say, "You are an individual who really does matter! You are unique!"

I remember a very quiet and shy boy in my Young Life club in Colorado Springs. One day he told me that he had decided to become a follower of Jesus, and he had invited the Lord into his life. I asked him what had led to that wonderful decision. His answer had a profound impact upon me. He said, "When you learned my name." It seemed that most people did not bother to learn his name. He was one of those forgotten kids who had quietly faded into the landscape—not a leader or a popular kid. I decided right then to try never to forget the first and last name of any young person I ever met. At least this is one way to say, "You are important as an individual. You really matter!" This is *recognition*!

We know also that young people wish to give themselves to something, or to someone. As a result they may get involved in destructive behavior, or associate with less-than-desirable characters or activities. More positively, they may take up a cause or get involved in athletics, music, or drama. But it is one of the four wishes of a young person to give themselves. There is a built-in need to be involved in something, whether it is good or bad. Their self-worth may be on the line. Here we observe the wish for *response*!

There is nothing so meaningful for anyone as feeling loved. Will those young people you work with have that life-changing, immeasurable experience? Pray that Jesus will share his love through you with all those young people you meet. For them it will mean a new sense of *security*!

It seems that there is a built-in wish for many young people to "try stuff." Some things are not productive, but may be part of their culture. Kids often get into drugs and alcohol because of their curiosity, as well as social pressures. This, and other behavior may mostly be about a wish for *the new experience*!

I want to encourage you in any way I can toward becoming a student of the adolescent culture. It is all a part of incarnational witness. We are continuing the incarnation of Jesus when we love kids with this level of sensitivity and understanding!

God bless you as you reach those wonderful young people right where they live!

I'll stay in touch.

Mitch

Reaching A Diverse World

Dear Young Life Leader,

Today I want to write you about an important value of Young Life: We are committed to racial diversity and equality.

Young Life's early history was white, suburban, upper- and middle-class kids. That's who it started with and that's who it was. It continued that way for many years.

As you probably know, things began to change in our culture in this country in the late 1950s and throughout the 1960s. There were protests and riots as our black citizens struggled for equality. Young Life found itself in the middle of this. Over time we realized that this mission, if it were to be true to its calling to reach all kids with the gospel of Jesus, we had to deal with some of these issues.

On one side of the spectrum were people who said we should not waste our time with this effort. There were even some donors who said that if we had black kids in camp they would no longer send their own kids nor support Young Life anymore.

On the other side of the spectrum you had some prophetic voices within Young Life. People like George Sheffer, Bill Winston, Verley Sangster, Harv Oostdyck, Bill Milliken, and Bo Nixon, as well as Dean Borgman, Jim Hornsby, and Bud Ipema. Like all prophets, they were ahead of their time and, to be honest, were often hard to take. But they pulled us, sometimes kicking and screaming, to a better, more biblical place.

Please understand: All of this was very painful. People on both sides of the issue had strong feelings and could be very passionate, sometimes to the point of some downright unchristian behavior on all sides. We made mistakes along the way. My gut tightens up even now all these years later as I think back on those times. It was a struggle in every sense of the word.

For those of us who wanted to expand Young Life's reach, our argument was simple. "Go and make disciples of all nations" includes the inner city as well as it does the suburbs, doesn't it?

The gospel itself does not exclude anyone. The only ticket required is belief, not a particular income or skin color.

We realized that we could no longer be an all-white organization, and frankly, we were the better for the change. Our urban brothers and sisters gave us a better and more full understanding of the gospel and how it's for every part of the world. They also helped us expand our understanding of the universal Church. At a time when we could have rested on our laurels, they encouraged us to keep moving and growing. It was a social and spiritual correction for our mission that brought us more in line with what Jesus wanted for us.

My friend, I hope that wherever you are, that you are open to taking God's message of the gospel to everyone and to learning from brothers and sisters in Christ who may look different from you. What we have in common is not external, it is Jesus.

Yours in him,

Mitch

Women in Ministry

Dear Young Life Leader,

Young Life was blessed from the very beginning with strong, spiritual, capable leaders, several of whom were women. I'm thinking now of Wanda Ann Mercer, Annie Cheairs, Kay McDonald, Gladys Roche, Ollie Dustin, Janie (Harold) Sutherland, and others. They were outstanding and had a tremendous influence on all of us who were involved in Young Life at the time.

At the same time the urban battles were going on that I talked about in my last letter, our culture was also undergoing seismic shifts in the way that women were viewed in our society. The women I mentioned in the paragraph above grew up in a Christian subculture that said that women never were to give leadership to men—even though in many instances they were smarter, wiser, and more biblically-literate than some of us men.

During my tenure as President of Young Life, I became increasingly convicted—with some external prodding, I confess—that there is no biblical basis for withholding women from positions of leadership. My wife Claudia was a tremendous help to me as I began to think through all of this. While there were no women in the band of twelve apostles, even a simple reading of the Gospels reveals that some of Jesus' closest followers were women. In fact, while all the men took off from the cross, who stayed? Mark 15:40 gives us the answer: "Mary Magdalene, Mary the mother of James and of Joses, and Salome … Many other women who had come up with him to Jerusalem were also there."

I began to get angry letters, from both men and women, including some staff, when I began to push for a more equal role for women in our mission. They didn't feel it was right for Young Life to open up any and all positions of leadership to women. Getting those letters was difficult. Many of these people were friends and people I greatly respected.

On the other side of the fence we had some leading theologians, chief among them Paul Jewett, who convinced me and the rest of Young Life's leadership that, biblically speaking, it was time to open up the opportunities for women. "There is neither Jew nor Greek, slave nor free, male nor female, for you are all one in Christ Jesus" (Galatians 3:28).

Taken together, the issue of women in leadership and the struggles we had with expanding our urban outreach made for some very difficult days for me as President of Young Life. Not everyone agreed with the decisions I made, but the mission stuck to them. In all, I believe that all of this had a purifying effect on Young Life.

It thrills me today when I see women stand up in a Young Life club and proclaim the gospel with excellence, or when I visit a camp in the summer and see lots of high school kids from urban areas having the greatest week of their lives.

As you go about your work as a Young Life leader, don't shy away from having your convictions challenged. It may be difficult but you never know when the Lord might rattle your cage in a way that makes an eternal difference in the lives of others. Strive to be in line, not with our culture, but with the Holy Spirit!

Your brother in Christ,

Mitch

Kids with Disabilities

Dear Leader,

Until 1986 there was no concerted effort to go into the world of kids with disabilities. This is when the Capernaum effort began. In San Jose, California, Nick Palermo was given the vision for this wonderful ministry which now spreads across the U.S. and a growing number of international locations.

I encourage you to be aware of Capernaum, and open to whatever involvement the Lord may wish for you to have. Especially do I encourage you to pray for kids with disabilities, and for those leaders who work with them. Most likely you will see young people with disabilities around the school where you are working in Young Life.

In light of the fact that close to twenty percent of the teen population has some form of disability, and that there are over six hundred million people with disabilities worldwide, we might ask, "what took us so long?"

I guess there are a number of answers to this question. Most have to do with our culture at large. These are young people who are threatening to a culture that worships at the altar of power, success, and appearance. Kids with disabilities just don't fit in many of our social structures. Instead of power there is weakness. Instead of success there is an inability to produce on levels desired by society. In appearance these are broken and sometimes disfigured bodies. I am referring specifically to kids with physical and/or mental disabilities. Many leaders in our society walk the other way or overtly reject this group of kids. They become invisible. Often there is a feeling of discomfort—leaders not knowing what to do or say.

In church youth groups and in Young Life, we experience the fear of the unknown. What do I do? What do I say? How do I talk with someone who is nonverbal? How could I possibly include them in my program and make it all work?

These are all barriers erected by us and not by kids with disabilities themselves. Their greatest disability may, in fact, be those able-bodied people who are afraid, or unwilling, to engage with them in some meaningful way.

Nick met kids with disabilities in 1980 on the Blackford High School campus. He had no background in all of this, and was terrified. He felt foolish and did not know what to do. God spoke a word to him clearly one morning as he read the parable of the Great Banquet in Luke 14:16–24. The word was, "Be comfortable with being uncomfortable." That broke the ice for him. Once he realized these were kids who happened to have disabilities, and not disabilities who happened to be kids, they became his friends.

And so as you encounter young people with disabilities in your area, the following realities are things Nick and other Capernaum leaders believe you should know. Perhaps the Lord is speaking to you about your personal involvement somehow with these wonderful kids.

- Young people with disabilities are like any other kids in most ways. They have the same hopes, dreams, and fears. They have the same longings—especially the desires to belong, to be valued, and to contribute with their lives.

- Treat them as you would wish to be treated, and as you would treat anyone else.

- You can find out how a certain kid communicates by talking with his or her parents, or a teacher.

- Discover what their unique needs are, and how to meet those needs. Again, you may talk with a parent or teacher for this information.

- Seek to help them fulfill their potential, as limited or extensive as that may be.

- Realize that these young people with disabilities are created in the image of God no less than you, having gifts, talents, and abilities to contribute. Take them seriously. They are not inferior as persons, and are dearly loved by God.

- Introduce your new friends with disabilities to your traditional club kids. Able-bodied young people will follow your leadership in becoming friends, and in becoming comfortable with being uncomfortable.

- Don't worry about the capacity of kids with disabilities to understand the gospel. This is not a problem for the Holy Spirit. These kids "get it" with their spirits, more so than with their minds.

- Bring discipline when it is needed. Set boundaries. You will be in a number of social situations when they will need help in relating properly with others.

- This is a ministry "with," as opposed to a ministry "to" kids. You will gain as much or more from young people with disabilities as you give them. Look for Jesus to show up in your relationships. When we minister to a young person with disabilities, in a very real sense we are ministering to Jesus himself. He stands that closely with these wonderful kids. Remember his words recorded in Matthew 25:40—"Whatever you did for one of the least of these brothers of mine, you did for me."

- For kids in wheelchairs you will need to work out their transportation requirements. Remember always to stay on eye-level with them in conversation. Respect their wheelchair just as you respect another person's body.

- Most importantly, may you realize how much Jesus loves kids with disabilities! The Gospels are filled with stories about people with physical challenges. Obviously they are a major priority with Jesus. They were not optional for him to care for, and neither are they for us in Young Life.

Not all leaders are called to work professionally with kids who have disabilities. But we are called to be their friends. So jump in, and become comfortable with being uncomfortable!

God bless you,

Mitch

Appreciating Donors

Dear Leader,

I wish to write today about one of Young Life's most valuable treasures: people around the mission who support it with their prayers and finances. Please see these donors as wonderful gifts from God, and treat them accordingly. We would not be where we are today without people who have cared enough about kids meeting Jesus to give their financial support to see it happen. It has always been that way.

I was uniquely privileged as a kid to witness how financial partnerships in ministry are formed. Jim came to my father and my uncle and asked them for money to finance the first Young Life event—the 1940 tent campaign. This was the beginning of a fabulous journey of faith for our family.

I remember what a joy it was for Mom and Dad over the years to be part of this wonderful enterprise with kids called Young Life. Never did I sense this to be for them an obligation in fulfillment of a pledge. It was an expression of who they were as believers who were fortunate enough to be in a position of trust by God to support a mission with kids around the world.

Young Life is what it is today because the Lord has raised up people of faith who want to see kids have a chance to hear the good news that "God so loved the world that he gave his only Son." When we review our history and recall the thousands of people who have carried this mission with their love and support we know we are on holy ground!

Let me suggest to you a few essentials in the care of donors. For starters, never take donors for granted! This means staying in touch, sharing the excitement of the ministry, as well as the challenges. Donors want to hear from you personally and directly. I loved it when Jim would come to our house and I could listen to him tell Mom and Dad his stories, as only he could, about the kids he was working with, those kids he was getting to know. I observed firsthand how glad Mom and Dad were to be involved in the inner workings of Young Life, and to be trusted to share in Jim's feelings. Make no assumptions that donors already know what is going on. They need to hear directly through you about the wonderful workings of God's grace.

Whenever possible let donors see Young Life in person. Nothing is more effective than having them see a camp or club in action. Especially is the adult guest program at the Young Life camps a beautiful way to let people see Young Life. They see leaders relating to kids and giving them a wonderful time, and they hear the gospel proclaimed so powerfully.

There are many wonderful stories of people becoming donors when they actually saw Young Life in action. Each of Young Life's camp properties has its own wonderful stories of God's blessing through donors who have seen Young Life in action as adult guests.

There are many ways to say "thank you" to people who give to the mission. Use them all—personal visits, phone calls, electronic messages, regular mail, or whatever is available to you. And always may the set of your heart be thankfulness as you pray regularly for your donors.

Tell donors the real-life stories of the ministry. Talk about kids. You don't have to mention their names if this is privileged information, or things young people have shared with you in confidence.

Treat donors as you would wish to be treated yourself. Didn't Jesus say something like that? "Do unto others as you would have them do unto you"?

Praying for you,

Mitch

Innovation
and Creativity

Dear Leader,

One of the things Young Life has always celebrated is the tremendous creativity of its staff. Those early folks were creative by necessity—no one had ever thought of having an evangelistic ministry centered around the high school, whose primary audience was to be kids who didn't know Jesus. This was all new ground.

For many years everything Young Life did was on an experimental, trial-and-error basis. First were the tent campaigns, followed by mass meetings and rooftop rallies at hotels. Then came the club meetings like the one that met in my home. All of this was "from scratch." When something didn't work or was seen to be outdated, those pioneers figured something else out. If we hadn't been encouraged to evaluate and think through things and innovate, Young Life would still be doing rooftop rallies and literature distribution and having dueling concert pianos at mass meetings!

Jim used to tell us, "The best Young Life work has yet to be done"—and he meant it. He always wanted us to be looking for new and better ways to gain a sympathetic hearing for the gospel with kids.

Nowhere in my own life was creativity and innovation more called upon than when I had the privilege of creating the program for Malibu Club in Canada. It was our fourth camp, after the three Colorado ranches—Star, Silver Cliff, and Frontier. We'd never had a water camp, only landlocked ranches (in fact, what is now known as the Properties Department was simply called "the ranches" until Malibu came along).

So what in the world would you do with a property that was surrounded on three sides by water and one side by mountain, had no horses, and sat on only a few acres of land? To make matters more complicated, the inlet's water was constantly flowing, either in or out, with the tide, often creating a downright dangerous environment. Sometimes the best creativity is when your hand is forced. We may not have had horses, but we had lots and lots of water. So we came up with all sorts of water-related activities.

When the ship of new campers would round the point heading into camp we sent out our fastest speed boat with our best water-skier. He would circle the ship on one ski, waving and greeting the ship-full of campers.

We also made up an event we called The Regatta, basically a parade on water. The event was started by a band made up of whatever musicians we had in camp. Playing John Philip Sousa marches, they passed the judges's stand and their fearless drum major (staff man Tom Bade) would lead them—right off the dock and into the water, blowing their horns the whole way down.

Kids decorated large rowboats with whatever items they could find (we didn't provide anything for them). They would choose a queen from among their members and seat her on a throne in the middle of the boat. Then the boats would float past the reviewing stand made up of adult guests who would determine who had the best float while each team cheered on their entrant. (While all this was going on—and the Regatta and related competitions would take two hours—one kid from each team would be chosen as their team's fisherman. That poor kid would have to sit by himself at the end of the dock while all the fun was going on and try to catch the most fish.)

Sometimes circumstances stretched our creativity to the hilt. That first summer it seemed like it rained every day and we had to reinvent the program on the fly.

The harbor master was the person who was in charge of all of our various boats. In one of those early summers the harbor master was a college kid, Bill Johnson, who knew boats quite well. At that time we only had one ski boat, but it was our pride and joy. Bill drove that boat for hours each day, hauling skiers around.

One day Bill was servicing the engine of the ski boat, by himself, in the middle of the inlet. For reasons hard to explain, he was thrown out of the boat while the engine was racing at full speed. We watched transfixed from the shore as the boat went around and around in seemingly endless circles, around Bill in the 25-fathoms-deep water. We didn't have any idea how we were going to stop that boat.

Physics took over and handled the situation for us. The boat was making wider and wider circles and, as we watched on, helpless, that beautiful speed boat, our only ski boat, rammed into the shore, disintegrating into a million pieces. (By the way, in our shock we had forgotten about poor old Bill, treading water in the middle of the inlet. Finally we heard a small voice, far off, yelling, "Help!" We quickly dispatched a rowboat to save him.)

Needless to say, we had to get creative the rest of that summer until we could get a new boat. Somehow, between all of us on the assigned team, we were always able to come up with games and activities that ensured kids had a great time, even if those activities weren't listed in the camp brochure!

What a great gift that was to me to have to create an entire program from scratch! I treasure those memories.

I hope you are getting to express your God-given creativity in all sorts of ways in Young Life. Let me encourage you, if you ever get a weekend or summer camp program assignment to approach it as I had to at Malibu—from scratch. How would you design a camp program for today's kids? Don't assume there are any sacred cows. Be willing to experiment!

In the same way, I hope you approach your club talks and Campaigner lessons with innovation and creativity. All of us in my generation of staff members began our speaking careers imitating Jim's messages (as Jim himself had imitated his father, who was an evangelist of some note). But—and this is important—as we grew in our own faith and deepened our personal experience with Jesus—we wrote our own messages that we were able to deliver with heartfelt conviction, because they were just that— our *own* messages.

There are so many outlets for creativity within the mission of Young Life. Please seek to honor our Creator by being creative in them. Evaluate events. Ask why messages or programs or schedules did or did not work. Question why certain things are done, and don't be afraid to experiment.

There is, of course, a difference between imitation and creativity. I encourage you to be creative! What a joy it is to serve the Lord with the gifts he has given us—and he has given all of us, including you, a creative spirit.

Sincerely in Christ,

Mitch

— Letter 22 —

Training in Young Life

Dear Leader,

When I graduated from college and decided to join the Young Life staff in 1949, Jim sent me, along with Bill Starr and Van Nall, to complete the graduate biblical studies program of Multnomah School of the Bible in Portland, Oregon. Jim knew that we needed biblical training to prepare us for being on the Young Life staff. My degree in Physics definitely would not cut it. This emphasis upon biblical training was to continue in ensuing years.

The first formal training program for staff was the "Station Wagon Institute" in the early 1950s. The small number of new staff drove together in a station wagon to study for two weeks at a time with various professors across the country.

This program was followed by the Young Life Institute, which was formed for training staff in theology, biblical studies, and speech. It was held first at Star Ranch and later at Fountain Valley School in Colorado Springs. Staff came for study during the summer months. The program was led by Dr. Paul Jewett of Fuller Theological Seminary.

In 1966, Bill Starr, by then the President of Young Life, asked me to move to Colorado Springs to be the Director of Training for the mission. I loved that assignment, largely because I knew there was a great need for training among the staff and volunteers. I was given free reign to develop the training program. I knew I needed academic assistance in this task. That need was met with a gifted individual, Dr. Darrell Guder. With Darrell the Institute for Youth Ministries—the IYM—became Young Life's excellent training program, done in partnership with Fuller Theological Seminary.

As you do your ministry with kids I hope you will seek always to grow in your knowledge of Scripture, in the practice of spiritual disciplines, and in your understanding of what ministry with young people is all about. Do you feel prepared in these areas? Have you received, or are you receiving, training in such disciplines as Old and New Testament studies, biblical theology, the content of the gospel, the culture of the adolescent, the preparation and delivery of a Young Life message, the relationship of Young Life with the Church, and in other important areas of training and leadership?

The reason I am telling you all this history is that I wish to underscore how important training has been over the years. Please follow through diligently in your training for the Young Life staff. This may be through the Young Life training program or through a seminary education. (If you are a volunteer leader you should receive training through your local area and your region.)

Please take advantage of whatever resources are available to you to prepare yourself theologically and in the practice of the mission. Be relentless in your pursuit of training!

May the Lord lead you in this journey of preparation,

Mitch

Section Four

— Finally … —

Don't Ever Let 'Em Quit Talking About Jesus

Jim Rayburn died on December 11, 1970. He was sixty-one years old, living the last days of his life at home in Colorado Springs while battling cancer. We had some wonderful conversations together in those last months, and even as he lay dying there were beautiful touches of his ever-present humor as we recounted experiences of the years together in Young Life.

A holy moment was given to me in one of those days. Knowing the time was short, I took the opportunity to thank him for leading so many of us to Jesus. It was one of the few times I remember Jim being totally at a loss for words. I could only guess what he was feeling.

He then gave me an admonition I shall never forget as long as I live. We were talking about the imperatives of the gospel, and that all kids need to hear the good news of Jesus Christ. To emphasize his point, Jim reached over to his bedside table and found an envelope and pen. He began to scribble a short list of words he entitled, "The Finished Work of Christ." He listed theological terms like "justification," "redemption," "sanctification," and "propitiation."

Showing the envelope to me he said, "*That's* what we are all about, Mitch. *Don't ever let 'em quit talking about Jesus!*"

"Don't ever let 'em quit talking about Jesus!" When the man who has been instrumental in bringing you and countless thousands of others to Jesus makes a statement like that, you can never be the same. Ministry takes on an entirely new dimension. I can still hear him say those words in his quiet, deliberate, impassioned style. I pray they will resound always throughout Young Life, as long as this mission exists!

"Don't ever let 'em quit talking about Jesus!"

If I had to pick out the one most important historic value in Young Life it would be its radical commitment to the gospel of Jesus Christ, as it is expressed in the Incarnation event. "God became flesh and lived among us" (cf. John 1:14).

I first heard that message in the old circus tent in 1940. For whatever reasons, the huge majority of kids back then didn't know the first thing about a personal relationship with God. God seemed far off, and certainly did not factor into our activities, or even into our thinking.

The same seems to be true for most teenage young people today. Even with technology and communication capabilities reaching an all-time high in our world, somehow our kids are missing the essential message of hope and life that only can be found in Jesus. For so many, the pace and demands in the adolescent culture have crowded faith off the screen of everyday life.

Our message to kids often begins with the question, "If there is a God, as many of us believe there is, what is this God like?" Then we may list a few ideas we have heard young people express concerning this question.

"God is a vague concept, and far distant from my activity and being."

"How can there be a God of love when there is so much suffering in the world?"

"Why are there so many ideas about God, with everyone thinking they are right?"

To those questions, and many more, we turn to the Incarnation event, when God answered eternal questions with his very presence on earth. Here we are at the heart of the gospel, and the Young Life message. Scripture teaches, "Christ Jesus[,] who being in very nature God, did not consider equality with God something to be grasped, but made himself nothing, taking the very nature of a servant, being made in human likeness. And being found in appearance as a man, he humbled himself and became obedient to death—even death on a cross!" (Philippians 2:6–8).

The message of Jesus climaxes with the incomparable story of his death and resurrection, assuring forgiveness and preparing the way of salvation for all of humankind. It is a moment of eternal truth when kids are given the chance to accept the gift, and, for all eternity, to love the Giver!

"Don't ever let 'em quit talking about Jesus!"

The whole of biblical revelation, starting from the Old Testament right through to its climax in Jesus Christ, proclaims this one exciting and meaningful message: God is not just a nondescript impersonal power; rather, like me, God is a person who knows and loves, and offers me a personal friendship.

"Don't ever let 'em quit talking about Jesus!"

In Young Life's proclamation of the incarnation of God in Jesus there may have been an area of weakness. Most leaders have been effective in teaching on the deity of Christ—that

Jesus is fully God. The miracle accounts in the Gospels have provided powerful proof of that reality. But equally important is the humanity of Christ. He feels what we feel, and is tempted in every way we are. He didn't manage to float through his life on earth about a foot off the same ground we walk on. The writer of Hebrews makes that abundantly clear, "For we do not have a high priest who is unable to sympathize with our weaknesses, but we have one who has been tempted in every way, just as we are—yet was without sin" (Hebrews 4:15). Is the Jesus we present to kids one who "feels" with us, and is not isolated from the difficult experiences we have in life? Let us then be careful to proclaim a Jesus who is fully and completely human. Yes, he changed water into wine, but also one day on a hillside he wept over a city of people in need.

"Don't ever let 'em quit talking about Jesus!"

There were many years in the mission when at the new staff training conferences we required the new staff to memorize a classic text on the Incarnation. These men and women left that gathering understanding what the mission is truly about! At the conclusion of the conference we would all stand together and quote in unison Colossians 1:15–20:

> Now Christ is the visible expression of the invisible God. He existed before creation began, for it was through him that everything was made, whether spiritual or material, seen or unseen. Through him, and for him, also, were created power and dominion, ownership and authority. In fact, every single thing was created through, and for, him. He is both the first

principle and the upholding principle of the whole scheme of creation. And now he is the head of the body which is the Church. Life from nothing began through him, and life from the dead began through him, and he is, therefore, justly called the Lord of all. It was in him that the full nature of God chose to live, and through him God planned to reconcile in his own person, as it were, on earth and everything in Heaven by virtue of the sacrifice of the cross." (J. B. Phillips translation)

What a magnificent and unforgettable experience this was each year!

For forty years while on the Young Life staff I would have the privilege of proclaiming this gospel. It was God's loving and mysterious way of giving to me a most wonderful opportunity to live out those powerful never-to-be-forgotten words of Jim in his final admonition to me. And like followers of Jesus all over the world, this gospel continues to sink ever deeper into my heart and life!

What is God like? Let the entire world of young people see him! His name is Jesus!

Don't ever quit talking about Jesus!

— Letter 23 —

Love the Gospel

Dear Leader,

I've given a lot of club talks over the years. The first time I got to speak at a weekend Young Life camp was when I was in college—way back in 1948 or so! That's a long time ago. I had the privilege to speak to high school crowds in the forties, fifties, sixties, seventies, eighties, and even a time or two in the nineties.

I know the culture is changing—it always is and always has been in a state of flux. Sometimes you may feel like there is nothing from the past that is relevant to today. But the gospel does not change, nor does its impact, and nor does what makes a message that God will be pleased to use.

We are told in Acts 14 that Paul and Barnabas "spoke in such a way that a great number of both Jews and Greeks believed" (Acts 14:1, ESV). Let us consider what it takes to speak "in such a way" that a great number will believe. H. A. Ironside pointed out that, "if it is possible to so speak that a multitude will believe, it is possible to so speak that nobody will believe! It is possible to preach so as to convert nobody."

It seems to me that there are two elements that are the most important in terms of effectiveness when presenting the gospel, and they both concern the presenter.

First, the man or woman who has the privilege of speaking to a group of kids is most effective when he or she knows those kids and when those kids know that their leader cares about them. I hope the importance of that has been made clear to you in these letters and in your own Young Life experience.

The second element for effective proclamation is that the presenter needs to know the message. That's what I really want to address in this letter. By knowing the message I don't just mean the specific talk he or she is going to give that night; I mean the gospel message itself. You need to become an expert in the gospel. You are never more attractive and winsome (to use an old Young Life word) as when you are confident about what you are saying.

Do you love the gospel? I'm not asking if you know a canned presentation of it. I'm asking if you *love* it? Do you study the four Gospels as if your life depends on them—because it does! Do you study the Scriptures and constantly wonder at the beauty of God's message of grace and love? Have you lingered over Galatians and Romans and marveled at the doctrine of salvation?

You remember I wrote you earlier about some of the theological terms Jim wrote down for me in his last days—words like *sanctification* and *propitiation*. Do you know what those words mean? If not, I encourage you to study deeply for yourself the finished work of Christ and never take for granted its unspeakable significance.

Continue always to study the Scriptures. Commit them to your heart in memory. Become a student of the gospel, ever-learning and contemplating the message of Christ.

What I am speaking about is true around the globe in every culture and was just as effective in 1948 as it was in 1998—even though the world changed unbelievably in the fifty years I was speaking before kids. And it is still effective today.

When you are confident in the message you don't need fancy props or the latest technology. You just need passion. And not a borrowed passion where you are merely mimicking a speaker you have heard before. Your message must be from the heart— *your* heart!

We were certainly captivated by the style and humor of those early Young Life speakers. They were very engaging. But the two things that made the greatest impact were the conviction with which they spoke, and the certainty of their love for us. It was and is a phenomenal combination.

I pray that you only grow deeper in your passion for the gospel. I know full well that as you do, that passion will flow over in your effectiveness in sharing the greatest news the world will ever know.

Yours in Christ,

Mitch

Talking about *ſ*in

Dear Young Life Leader,

I want to look with you today at one part of our gospel proclamation—the so-called "sin talk." This is the message that deals with our need for a Savior.

I wish to relate to you what I heard from all the early Young Life leaders as they shared the gospel with us in clubs and camps. These are some of the truths we learned and the feelings we had as we listened to those talks.

Usually they started with the fact that there is a God, who created our world, and he did it with perfection.

When he created human beings, once again he did it with perfection. Adam and Eve enjoyed their unbroken relationship with God and the universe.

God gave us free will. We can make choices. Influenced by the enemy of God, Adam and Eve chose to disobey God, and thus, sin entered the world. An important verse, teaching this truth, is Romans 5:12—"Therefore, just as sin entered the world through one man [Adam], and death through sin, and in this way death came to all men, because all sinned."

We were asked to look at our broken world, and also to look within ourselves. We saw how we messed up. We saw illustrations to which we could relate—right where we lived! We knew we were sinners! George Sheffer, one of the first staff, would say, "I'm not standing here yelling at you that you are all a bunch of sinners. I am standing *with* you saying, 'We all are sinners—each of us!'" And then he would quote Romans 3:23—"For all have sinned and fall short of the glory of God."

I never felt that leaders were talking down to us, or trying to lay a heavy guilt trip on us, but I knew I was disobedient toward God, and living a self-centered existence. It was all about me. My relationship with God was broken. We saw a graphic picture of a broken world, in which we were living participants. During those talks we were encouraged to look inward, and to look honestly.

But always there was a feeling that something wonderful lay ahead for us to hear—some really good news! Even in a message about sin there was an undefined atmosphere of hope!

We were about to hear the amazing and inclusive words of forgiveness for all people, through the redemptive sacrifice of Jesus on the cross! We would soon hear spoken with unforgettable God-given power the truths of Romans 5:8—"But God demonstrates his own love for us in this: While we were still sinners, Christ died for us." And we would hear 1 John 2:2—"He is the propitiation for our sins, and not for ours only but also for the sins of the whole world" (ESV).

Even though sin has broken our relationship with God we learned that we were not separated from his eternal love. A favorite story was the Prodigal Son text in Luke 15:11–31. The son was already forgiven through the grace of the father, not by anything the son did. All he had to do was come home and receive his father's forgiveness. We went out of those club meetings knowing we were forgiven. How could we not love Jesus and give our lives to such a one! And many of us did.

When we speak with young people about their sin, let us do so with humility and grace. Their repentance will come about when they understand that they are forgiven through the loving sacrifice of Jesus Christ on the cross. There is no need to hammer them with guilt. Always remember the prayer of Jesus on the cross, "Father, forgive them … they don't know what they are doing."

It's all about amazing grace!

Thankfully,

Mitch

Numbers in Their Proper Place

Dear Young Life Leader,

Does God care about numbers? How many there are of this or that, how big or small something is? How important to God are numbers?

Henrietta Mears, a churchwoman who was highly influential with a lot of us in the 1950s, used to laughingly point out that God cared a lot about numbers—he even wrote a whole book about it!

God is indeed a measurer: We know, for instance, the number of fish in the post-resurrection catch (153), we know how much food was left over after the feeding of the 5,000 (12 baskets full). Jesus told us that the Father even knows the very number of hairs on our heads!

So, yes, God is into the details. Along those same lines he expects his followers to keep honest books and records (see, for instance, Proverbs 11:1 and 16:11). I am proud of the work that pioneers like John Carter, our longtime director of finance for Young Life, and so many of our Board members did to keep Young Life "above board" in all matters of finances and accounting.

And Jesus also had an eye for large numbers of people. Our Lord was moved when he gazed upon the crowds. It broke his heart as he saw the masses, "bewildered and miserable" (J. B. Phillips translation), and he longed to be their shepherd (Matthew 9:36). When he looked upon Jerusalem (Luke 13:34) he said, "How often I have longed to gather your children together, as a hen gathers her chicks under her wing." (It is fascinating to me to see that Christ uses both masculine and feminine images for himself—a shepherd and a hen. He was not afraid in a patriarchal society to compare himself with that most matriarchal of all symbols, a mother hen!)

But we have to be careful when it comes to numbers. We used to remind ourselves to never count conversions because our number would be different from heaven's! If you've ever counseled kids at camp you know how true this is: some kids stand up at "Say-So" who haven't met the Lord, while others who have, don't!

My generation was incredibly competitive, whether it be in sports or the number of kids we could get to clubs and camp. There were times when you received recognition for the number of kids you had involved. We were praised when we did well— mostly informally, but that was where we got a lot of our value. There's nothing new about desiring large numbers in your ministry, whether it be for good, godly motives or bad, selfish ones.

As you know, at one point when I was running a Young Life club in Colorado Springs the Lord blessed that club with some rather astounding numerical growth. Club got so big that we had to hold the meetings in mortuaries around town. Young Life in a mortuary, how do you like the sound of that? I have to be honest and admit that my ego enjoyed that "success." But more than the numbers, I was excited about *who* some of those kids were: many of those kids were troublemakers, kids who were really outside of the faith. Sadly, I don't know whatever became of many of those kids, but it thrilled me then to look out on that room and know that these great kids were hearing the gospel.

Does God care about numbers? Yes, but only as those numbers represent individual people, individuals whom he loves uniquely, just as he created them uniquely.

May the Lord bless you this day—

Mitch

Timeless

Dear Young Life Leader,

Have you ever considered what makes Young Life unique? It's obviously a ministry that you have chosen to be a part of. Maybe it's a ministry that had a direct impact on your own young life growing up. But so many of us who have given our lives to this mission have never really stopped to consider what are the real essentials of this method that God revealed to those early leaders. So often we are too busy doing it to really think about it! But I want to encourage you to think about this a little bit today.

What helped a lot of us really consider this question was when Young Life first began to expand internationally. Those original brave pioneers were a delightful couple, Rod and Fran Johnston. God had laid it on their hearts to reach the youth of France and so, in 1953, off they went to Paris to get Young Life started.

Quickly, it became apparent to the Johnstons that kids in France were hungry for the very same thing that kids in the States were hungry for: meaningful relationships with caring adults who took the time to share the gospel with them in a way they could understand (in this case, in French!).

By the time I became President of the mission about twenty-five years later, Young Life had a presence not just in France, but Brazil, Canada, Bermuda, the Philippines, Australia, Germany, Korea, and a few other countries. Today Young Life's reach has continued a beautiful presence around the globe, and I give God the glory for that.

Every time we would help introduce Young Life-style ministries in these countries it was a reminder to us of what really made something "Young Life." It wasn't the clubs or camps or even the name—most of these outreaches went by names other than "Young Life."

No, what made something Young Life, whether it was in the high-income neighborhoods in France or the heartbreaking slums of São Paulo, was leaders—just like you—establishing relationships of love and trust with young people outside the faith and using those relationships to communicate the gospel of Jesus Christ to a hurt and broken world.

That is Young Life. And it works in every culture. This should come as no surprise to us as it was the same method our Lord used: "Look at him," the Pharisees said with disgust. "He eats with publicans and sinners!" (cf. Luke 5:30). Over and over again in the Gospels we see the same thing: Jesus—building relationships with "sinners." There were no camps or club meetings, no T-shirts, special musicians, or gimmicks. There was Jesus, loving those on the outside.

Jim Rayburn used to expound to us on Colossians 4:5: "Walk in wisdom toward them that are without" (KJV)—"without" being an old-timey word meaning "outside." "*That's* who we want to reach," he would thunder. "Young Life is not about reaching kids in the church, it's about reaching those kids who are on the outside. And there's only one way to do that. Jesus taught us by example: 'And the Word was made flesh, and dwelt among us, (and we beheld his glory, the glory as of the only begotten of the Father,) full of grace and truth' (John 1:14, KJV). They're not going to go to anything advertised 'Christian.' We have to go to them and build personal relationships of trust. Walk alongside them, listen to them, care for them."

We continue that incarnation internationally today. We go to be among them all around the world. My friend Bob Reeverts headed this effort for years and taught us so much.

Just a month ago as I write this letter in the summer of 2012, Claudia and I were given the opportunity to speak at a camp in Wales to the Young Life team working in the various nations of the United Kingdom and Scandinavia. Several countries were represented. What a joy it was to hear them share exciting reports of the great work God is doing through them in their countries with kids who don't know the Good News.

It works in every culture. It worked for Claudia and me in those early Dallas clubs in the 1940s as we went from being "without" the Christian faith to "within," and it is working today, over seventy years later, with kids in dozens of countries who are, in the words of Ephesians 2:12, "without hope and without God in the world."

I am so thankful for what you are doing—whether it be in an American suburb or somewhere in a Third World country. Be encouraged. Keep at it. Walk in wisdom toward those precious ones who are outside the faith.

Love in Christ,

Mitch

The Love of Jesus Compels Us

Dear Leader,

What keeps us going in our ministry with young people? What helps us in times of discouragement or doubt? We all have our days when very little good seems to be happening with the kids we seek to befriend. They may seem distant and not particularly interested in allowing us to enter their world. Over the years I remember some difficult times as a leader seeking to build relationships with unresponsive kids.

The Apostle Paul experienced hard times in his ministry with the people of Corinth. His letters reveal the pain of divisions among them and their misunderstandings of the gospel. What kept him going? I believe we have his answer in 2 Corinthians 5:14–15: "For Christ's love compels us ... he died for all, that those who live should no longer live for themselves but for him who died for them and was raised again." The love of Jesus kept Paul going. He used a very strong Greek word, *sunehei* (compels), to describe how the love of Jesus truly was the driving force in his life.

I pray that you as a leader will be sustained and motivated by the love of Jesus. It is a two-way love, his love for you, and in return, your love for him. "We love because he first loved us" (1 John 4:19). This is the heart of true ministry. We do what we do out of the compelling love of Jesus.

Our love grows as we encounter Jesus in prayer and in the daily experience of his presence. The more we see and hear him, the more we love him. And wonder of wonders, he causes his love to flow through us to those very kids who may be obnoxious, or seem not to care. You will do what you do, not because of your great love for teenagers, but because of his love for them, which is living in and through you.

So in those times when your ministry seems to be a drag, or when kids are unresponsive, remember the love of Jesus that compels (*sunehei*) you! In the mystery of the providence of God, he will love all those kids through you!

God bless you as you love kids with the love of Jesus!

Mitch

The Impact of Relational Ministry

[Editor's note: Nothing is more meaningful for a leader than hearing from an old "club kid" who had definitely been on the outside. After so many letters from Mitch, we thought a letter to him might be in order. This letter is from Randy Giusta, senior area director for Young Life in San Diego. It is offered here as a testimony to the power of relational ministry.]

Dear Bob and Claudia,

You probably remember Beth Sheppard who had been very involved with the Mira Monte High School Young Life club along with Bob and Terry Martin. As a senior, Beth was a club "Secretary," and Bob Martin was club "President." Beth told her freshman brother that he was going to Young Life. Mark said he would go, but only if he could bring a friend, and Beth agreed. So, I was asked to go to Young Life the fall of 1963, and was offered a ride from a pretty senior girl. What could I say? Of course, any excuse to get out of the house, and the invitation made me feel really special.

Now, before I get to my first club, I need to let you know why it was so appealing to "get out of the house." My parents divorced when I was nine, after years of violent fighting. My mom had left my dad to marry a self-proclaimed atheist. My mom hated religion, and was disgusted that my dad would take us to Mass a couple of times a month. Both my mom and dad were alcoholics from as early as I can remember. The first time I remember getting drunk was when I was five, going around at one of the parties at our home, finishing off the beer cans that revelers would leave around our home. I thought this was normal, until I was in my teens. When I started meeting other families, I began to see that my family was not the norm. Twenty years later I took a twelve-week class for Adult Children of Alcoholics, and they had us draw a family tree, labeling each person's addictions and dysfunctions. I quickly learned that I had a family "weed," not a family "tree."

So you see, I was outside of Christ's community of believers, and I had no encouragement from home to pursue faith of any kind, other than my dad's guilt of raising his kids in the Catholic tradition. So, when Mark and Beth took me to Young Life, it was a pivotal event for me. First, I was *invited* to come, not *told* to come. That is significant. Someone wanted me to go with them.

When I arrived at club, you were standing at the door welcoming everyone, and you looked me in the eye and asked me my name, and you welcomed me to Young Life with a *big,* goofy smile. I had so much fun, and something grabbed me at the end of club, when you started to talk about Jesus. It was important what you said, but what I remember is *how* you said it. You talked about Jesus like he was real, and you clearly were taken by His remarkable character. Your love for Christ was captivating. I sensed your passion, and listened to every word that you shared. I was mesmerized by the love and the truth that I was hearing. I longed for it.

The next week I returned, and you remembered *my* name! You had me now. In four years, I never missed one club meeting. It was my retreat from the storm. My mom and step-dad were fighting and divorced by the end of my freshman year. My step-dad believed that every man should have a wife and at least one mistress. This did not go down well with his previous five wives, and my mom was not finding this to her liking, either. Her drinking was getting more and more frightening. My dad was popping uppers and downers, and drinking whiskey for his "cough." I was getting more and more violent, given to frequent rages and fist-fighting with friends and family. I began drinking more myself to escape from the pain.

At the end of my sophomore year, Bob, you and some others rounded up some campership, and paid most of my way to Malibu Club for my first summer camp experience. It was that August of 1965 that I too fell helplessly in love with my Savior, and surrendered my life to His care. You paved the way for me prior to this trip by inviting me to your house every Friday morning before school for Campaigners. I remember Claudia keeping your kids quiet and out of the room, so we could hear you share the Bible with us guys. I remember, and anticipated your phone call *every* Thursday night, reminding me to come to your home the next morning. I remember you coming to a tennis match at the high school, and cheering me on. I remember this most, because I never had my mom or dad come to any sports event that I did in four years of high school. You stepped in to that gap. I did Work Crew at Malibu the summer after I graduated, and that month had more impact on my life than anything else that I can remember. I grew deeper in my love for Christ, and developed a passion to serve Him, and to share His love for others.

Well, during my last two years of high school, I was becoming a different person. The Holy Spirit was transforming me from the inside out. I began to love my mom and dad, rather than resent them. I started to love my peers, and was able to help lead several of my friends to know Christ as I did. I was a volunteer leader for four years in college, and now I've been on staff for over forty years. I am still passionate about sharing Christ's love with kids who have never darkened the doorway of a church. I have a special soft spot in my heart for kids from divorced homes and substance and sexual abuse. In truth, my heart breaks, and I have a proper target for my anger, as I see the Enemy tearing kids' lives apart.

Because you loved a boy like me who was outside the fold and led me to my Shepherd, God has touched countless lives, and I am only one of so many you have invited into your hearts and home. My own sons are teachers and Young Life staff, reaching out to lost teenagers, and bringing them home to Christ. Thank you for infecting me with that passion. I am eternally grateful.

Randy

— Letter 29 —

Young Life
and One's Family

Dear Leader,

Claudia and I love getting to speak to groups of staff and leaders around the country, and often we'll have a question-and-answer time during those sessions. The number one area we receive questions about is what I would like to address in this letter: the balance between family and ministry.

Over the years I have observed repeated struggles among married leaders in their understanding of time priorities. They find themselves dealing with the question, "Which comes first, my marriage and family, or my ministry?"

The tensions most likely come about over the leader's schedule. A spouse may feel that his or her partner is putting ministry before marriage, or that family matters do not seem as important to a leader as his or her ministry with Young Life.

I know the tension personally. I was one of those who all too often made schedule decisions independently. Ministry usually would come first. I would take far too many speaking engage-ments, camp trips, and other meetings in the performance of the Young Life program. I'm not proud of that, and over the years have sought counsel to determine reasons why, and to work on the formation of priorities, schedule planning, and boundaries.

One of those counselors became a lifelong friend, Dr. Bill Nesbitt of Fairfield, California. (Bill ultimately served on the national Board of Young Life.) One day I asked him the ques-tion, "Which comes first, family or ministry?" His answer was, "Neither! God comes first!" In ensuing months he helped me to understand the implications of being a follower of Jesus who must determine his schedule prayerfully, establishing one's pri-orities and activities always in the presence of God. Bill assured me that this would be a lifelong struggle, particularly for a "doer" such as me. I might find it hard to turn down a major speaking opportunity because I realized at that time I was being gone from the family too much.

As the years have passed I have acknowledged to my family that I have been "over the top" in scheduling my Young Life activities. They have been gracious, and thankfully, have not been resentful of my performance tendencies. Nor have they been bitter toward ministry in general. Each of our kids is engaged in a Christian ministry themselves. I am so grateful for their forgiveness!

One of your greatest challenges in your marriage and family will be in how to live out each day the admonition and reflection of Philippians 1:20–21—"I eagerly expect and hope that I will in no way be ashamed, but will have sufficient courage so that now as always Christ will be exalted in my body, whether by life or by death. For to me, to live is Christ and to die is gain."

I think Bill Nesbitt was right! To live out the love of Jesus in one's family will be a lifelong opportunity and challenge. But it can be done if we approach the matter honestly and prayerfully. Please don't ignore the issues that confront you. Listen to the concerns of your spouse, and share your feelings to develop intimacy. Let your children know they are deeply loved and enjoyed. Spend quality time with them. Be honest with yourself and seek out your true motives for your ministry activities. Work together with your spouse in scheduling. Don't let there be surprises. Keep your spouse informed. Open communication is essential for all healthy relationships. Ask yourself, "Is my ego dictating my priorities and schedule?" Let your ministry reflect the power and love of the Holy Spirit who continues the work of Jesus through you.

Perhaps we are all vulnerable at the point of our families, but our Lord will enable us to walk through these issues as we journey together.

My prayers continue with you,

Mitch

Principles for Ministry

Dear Leader,

I would like to look with you today at some of the essential biblical principles for the Young Life ministry. They are found in 1 Corinthians 2:1–5. "When I came to you, brothers, I did not come with eloquence or superior wisdom as I proclaimed to you the testimony about God. For I resolved to know nothing while I was with you except Jesus Christ and him crucified. I came to you in weakness and fear, and with much trembling. My message and my preaching were not with wise and persuasive words, but with a demonstration of the Spirit's power, so that your faith might not rest on men's wisdom, but on God's power."

The great Apostle Paul did not depend upon human ability or eloquence in his proclamation of the gospel. This brilliant communicator acknowledged his limitations. We may be good speakers, but the gospel we proclaim comes directly from God. We must proclaim it with true humility and deep respect.

Unfortunately, some club or camp messages I have heard seemed to have a "light" feel to them. They had humor, catchy illustrations, and even film clips and videos, but were lacking in a sense that this was the Lord speaking ... a "thus saith the Lord" feel to the message. This is the reason why we physically hold the Scriptures in our hands, or project them on a screen. We want kids to understand from where this message is coming. They must know that these are not *our* ideas.

How many times we heard Billy Graham say these words, "The Bible says ..." And Jim Rayburn often would turn the pages of his Bible toward us in the audience, running his finger along the lines as he read them out loud. We had no doubt from where this message was coming!

This is not to say that in our technological age we should not use film clips or other vehicles or visuals in our messages. It's just that these are always to be helps toward understanding the gospel. Technology must never overpower the message. It is the Holy Spirit who makes the Scriptures come alive and it is that same Spirit who transforms lives.

Paul wished never to talk down to his audience, using some sort of "superior wisdom." Do kids have the sense that we are speaking "with" them, and not "to" them? Is there a vulnerability, transparency, and honesty in our presentation, speaking out of our own life journey? If we tell stories of our personal failures we do it not for its "shock value," but rather to identify with hurting kids.

Two times in this letter we hear the Apostle Paul saying, "I came to you," and once he said, "I was with you." This affirms the biblical basis for Young Life's relational approach in its ministry. We go where young people are, whether the shopping mall or the athletic field. We become good students of their culture. We do things with them. We build relationships. We get to know them, not in some superficial way, but what their home and school situations might be. A real relationship will enable them to open up to their fears, struggles, temptations, and joys. Across the bridge of unconditional friendships we are able to share Jesus. In doing this, we are continuing the incarnation of Jesus, who came into our world to express the love of God. We, then, enter the world of the young in order to continue that expression.

Verse 2 defines our message and our motivation for ministry: "I resolved to know nothing, except Jesus Christ and him crucified." We are about Jesus, and radical in our focus upon him. We proclaim his grace and forgiveness shown on the cross. It is our wonderful privilege to share with kids the person of Jesus, and how he is the "visible expression of the invisible God." In our proclamation we walk with him, live with him, listen to him, and ultimately we see his magnificent sacrifice upon the cross, accomplishing forgiveness of sin for all of humankind! We proclaim his resurrection from the dead, and his words of call to discipleship—"Follow me ... Remember, I am with you always." This amazing message comes alive through the power of the Holy Spirit.

Usually we do not think of the Apostle Paul as one who is "weak, fearful, and trembling," but here we discover his true feelings about his ministry in Corinth. This text is a gift to any of us who have looked at a high school, middle school, Capernaum group, inner city neighborhood, or international culture, and prayed for wisdom in how to reach those young people with the gospel. We feel overwhelmed with the task, finding ourselves in a very lonely place. So did Paul!

And now we hear the most important truths for anyone in ministry! We may be dynamic leaders with kids, with a growing and exciting program of clubs and camps, with volunteer leaders joining us in the ministry, with an area committee behind us, and finances provided. We thank the Lord for these gifts! But we call out to God, as did Paul, for a "demonstration of the Spirit's power." This is the great mystery of ministry. We know it when we see it. We know there is something special going on, far beyond human programming or talent. It is the work of the Holy Spirit, who reveals Jesus to the world!

This leads us to the great reality of our personal relationship with the Lord of the Universe. Our ministry must flow out of that relationship if it is to have an eternal quality about it. Paul knew that when he said, "I resolved to know nothing while I was with you except Jesus Christ ..." His ministry flowed from an inner conviction, and his intimacy with Jesus! In his second letter to the Corinthians he says, "Christ's love compels us!" (verse 5:14).

Jesus himself is our example. He often went off to be with his Father in prayer. He lived in total dependence upon the Father, doing nothing by his own will. Over and again we hear his words, "I do nothing of myself ..." In John 10:38 he said, "Understand that the Father is in me, and I in the Father."

Where Young Life is vulnerable may be at this point. Effective and lasting ministry must flow from the hearts of leaders who are responding daily to Christ's presence within them. It is through that presence that we reach out to needy kids. We acknowledge his presence and seek humbly to do the Father's will. This only is the work of the Holy Spirit. It cannot happen through human programs or organizational controls. It happens:

—When we listen to our Lord in our prayers.

—When we cooperate with Jesus to accomplish his purposes.

—When we admit our fears and weaknesses, expressing our dependence upon him.

It is then when the ministry will flow out of Christ's presence within us. Thanks be to God!

First John 1:3 says, "That which we have seen and heard declare we unto you ..." (KJV). Will the young people we minister with know that something special is going on in our lives? Will they recognize that we have been with Jesus? I sure hope so.

Praying for you,

Mitch

In Praise of
Unsung Heroes

Dear Friend,

Throughout these letters I have mentioned often Jim Rayburn, my Young Life leader, my friend, and of course, the founder of the mission. He was a spiritual giant and, though he had feet made of clay, he is worthy of every mention I've made.

But in this letter I want to spend just a few moments talking about some other folks who made tremendous contributions to Young Life. Chances are you've never heard of them. They are the unsung heroes of this ministry. Jim didn't run this thing by himself, and he wasn't just aided by those of us getting a paycheck from Young Life.

There are too many individuals and groups to mention by name, but the Lord has laid it on my heart to single out a few.

In addition to Jim and his wife Maxine, let us not forget the contributions of the other patriarchs of the mission and their wives: Add and Loveta Sewell, Wally and Esther Howard, and George and Martie Sheffer. I'm sorry that you've probably never heard their names, but they were right there, making unbelievable sacrifices and invaluable contributions to start a ministry that most around them did not understand or appreciate.

I must also mention the Board members I had the privilege to work with over the years, starting all the way back at the very onset of Young Life. You see, both my father, Orville, and my uncle John, served on the original Board of Young Life, and both served on the Board until their deaths many years later.

They were joined by men like E. M. Wetmore, H. J. Taylor, and Alex McKenzie. These were solid men of God, deeply devoted to their faith, committed churchmen, and business leaders of the highest integrity. You have to understand, in those days, Young Life was a nothing organization. Nobody had ever heard of it. And frankly, its methods were considered suspect by what felt like the majority of church leaders around the country.

Yet these men came alongside the early staff and leant their own credibility and a good deal of their treasure and gave Young Life a boost that only God could have ordained. They took their role seriously and spent tremendous amounts of time in prayer and study, always desiring that Young Life be true to the Scriptures.

Shortly after those very first years the Board was joined by a man who would become my close friend, C. Davis Weyerhaeuser. He was one of the greatest combinations of wealth and humility that I have ever known.

I don't want to continue naming names because you might get bored! But believe me when I tell you, my young friend, that Young Life would not be what it is today had it not been for these board men—and later, women—who gave of themselves to Young Life in the capacity that God had gifted them. They demanded excellence and integrity of us and made us the better for it.

Another group whose praises I wish to sing is all of those local committee members who have been such a vital part of what Young Life does. You know, in the earliest days, we didn't have local committees. Everything was staff-driven. It was a great day when God revealed to Bill Starr, then the area director of Portland and who later served as President between Jim and me, that areas should gather around themselves groups of local men and women to form what became known as Young Life committees.

In my own experience, no one has personified what a committee member could mean more than my great friend Ted Johnson. As I wrote you in an earlier letter, we met when we were young guys shortly after I arrived in the San Francisco Bay Area to become area director in 1956. Ted became my committee chairman. There wasn't a day that went by that I didn't talk to Ted by phone or in person. He brought a set of gifts that I didn't have. He understood the business world—he knew how businesspeople and donors thought. And he was a superb salesman—he knew what would sell. "Mitch, this won't fly," he might say, or "Mitch, you've got it!"

Ted and his beautiful wife Nancy became great friends for life with Claudia and me. We laughed together and prayed together. Ted made sure the whole Bay Area work was funded. I was the one up front, the one kids would remember, and the one who got whatever credit and plaudits there were to be had. I am here to tell you, though, that when Ted and I arrive in heaven—and it may not be long for either of us as we are now in our eighties—Ted is going to be overwhelmed by the rewards that he will receive, handed to him personally by Jesus.

There have been many great committee members like Ted who have served so faithfully and so well the mission of Young

Life. You may be one of them. If so, please know that your contribution does not go unnoticed. You make such a difference. I would encourage you to be like Ted: take your role seriously and with joy, and marvel at what Jesus does in the work of the ministry that you help support.

The last group I want to mention is maybe the most unsung group of all in Young Life, and certainly the most heroic. It's the staff wives—and now, staff spouses—who labor unheralded alongside the staff member to whom they're married.

My dictionary says that "long-suffering" means "having or showing patience in spite of troubles." Boy, does that describe the staff spouses I have known. It's not easy being married to a staff member of Young Life. The hours are crazy, the demands are nonstop, and the pay for field staff is never what it should be. It was always a goal when I was in Young Life's upper management to make life better for staff families, but it was a struggle and sometimes we just weren't able to pay our staff enough.

I know in my own life having Claudia by my side has made my sixty years of ministry possible. She has been more than a helper, she has been my partner in Christ. What a gift she is! The same is true for all of those long-suffering spouses out there. Thank you for freeing up your spouse to do what God has called him or her to do. Just as I could not have done it without Claudia by my side, I know they feel the same way.

So, here's to the unsung heroes of Young Life. Those beautiful folks who are so often behind the scenes making it all happen. Praise God for each one of them, and for you, too!

Yours in Christ,

Mitch

Camaraderie

Dear Young Life Leader,

There is something very special about relationships in Young Life. I can't explain it, but I know it is a reality. For seventy years I have witnessed friendships which were being formed for a lifetime. People were on a Work Crew together, or served in an area or region together, or had a summer assignment together. There is something unusual about what happens in situations like these. A "camaraderie" is formed.

Claudia and I have been privileged to continue our association with this mission all over the world. We love its style, its purpose, and especially its people. So many now are our friends! Some are our former club kids. Others are staff people we have gotten to know over the years. Some are faithful donors, or committee persons. What a tremendous fellowship it is!

Years ago Goldbrick, the first chef for Frontier Ranch, taught us some unforgettable lessons about fellowship. Hundreds of kids would be in camp, all of them hungry. As each day he and the Work Crew prepared huge quantities of food, often he would say cheerfully to his kitchen crew, "We're all in this together!"

That's it! That is the mystique and joy of Young Life. *We are in it together, to see that all kids the world over have a chance to know and follow Jesus.*

This is what the beloved apostle John was talking about when he said, "We proclaim to you what we have seen and heard, so that you also may have fellowship with us. And our fellowship is with the Father and with his Son, Jesus Christ" (1 John 1:3).

Many Young Life people have gone on to be with the Lord in heaven. Some were used greatly by God to shape this mission. Some were simple and faithful followers of Jesus. We will see them again in glory, along with those they influenced by their lives. What a joyful reunion it will be!

Thanks be to God!

Mitch

A Final Prayer

Dear Young Life Leader,

I wish now to offer a prayer for you as you involve yourself in this wonderful mission with kids. In his "Great Commandment," Jesus uses two very important words—"soul" and "strength" (Luke 10:27). These words teach us how we are to love God.

I am to love God with all of my soul. What does this mean? Psalm 103:1 describes the soul with these beautiful words, "Bless the LORD, O my soul: and all that is within me, bless his holy name" (KJV) Is not this a description of our souls—all that is within us? When we do "soul-searching" we go deep within ourselves. It is that place of "being." It is truly who we are as persons.

My prayer for you is that you will minister out of an intimate relationship with Jesus, captivated by his Holy Spirit. Only if ministry flows from this source, from a life of continuing prayer deep within us, will it be fruitful!

And I pray for strength in your wonderful journey. May this strength come not from organizational growth statistics, but rather may your strength be as the Apostle Paul expressed in 2 Corinthians 12:9—"made perfect [complete] in weakness." Humility is an essential characteristic of effective leadership at all levels of an organization. We minister out of our own weakness and sense of dependence upon our gracious Lord.

Let us hear with respect the timeless words of Nehemiah, "The joy of the LORD is your strength" (Nehemiah 8:10). Joy in Jesus has been one of Young Life's most attractive qualities. We laugh easily and thrill to tell stories of Jesus and his love.

Joy is rooted in our deepening understanding of our wonderful Savior, who loves us and gave himself for us. Joy is deeper than happiness, which is dependent on circumstance, and it is the hallmark of true believers throughout all time and regardless of situation or persecution. "These things have I spoken unto you, that my joy might remain in you, and that your joy might be full" (John 15:11, KJV).

May God bless you as you continue to share this Jesus with young people. It has been my privilege to serve alongside you.

Your brother in Christ,

Mitch

P.S.

— Spiritual Formation —

An Important Moment

This last section is a little different from the first four, but I encourage you to stick with it. Though it is characterized here as a postscript (or P.S.), the spiritual disciplines I describe herein have been of tremendous benefit to Claudia and me and I believe you will find them helpful too. To begin, I want to share how they became a part of my life.

My first staff assignment was to lead three Young Life clubs—Colorado Springs High School, Yuma High School, two hundred miles to the east, and Pueblo Centennial High School, forty miles to the south. (In the early days almost all of the staff led more than one club.)

The Colorado Springs club caught on, and often there were over three hundred kids in attendance each week, meeting in three funeral homes in town, the only few places large enough to hold that number. I loved it, and of course received plenty of affirmation. *A pattern was being established in my life, which continued for many years.*

Young Life staff had become quite competitive. We were affirmed for our "performances"—mostly for how many kids came to club, how many were active in Campaigners, and how many we took to camp. Also we received affirmation for our ability to give good talks, effectively using biblical texts concerning Jesus, with humor and an attractive style.

This "performance pattern" continued through the years of being a Regional Director, Divisional Director, U.S. Field Director, Training Director, and President. I loved those years, and thank the Lord for his hand of blessing upon the ministry!

The downside was that without being aware of the consequences I was finding my identity and self-worth in *what I did*, rather than in *who I was in relationship with Jesus*. I was too much about accomplishment and performance. It was fun and exciting to do the mission of Young Life. There was a downside. My family paid a price for my schedule and my insensitivity for being a husband and a father. My personal relationship with the Lord suffered as well.

About midway through my Young Life presidency I experienced a spiritual drought. I was teaching things about Jesus that I knew were true, but I was not experiencing them personally. The daily experience of intimacy with Jesus was missing in my life. Thinking things would get better, I buried myself in the activities and the myriad of responsibilities of the office. My solution would be my performance as a Christian leader. Soon I discovered this to be a dead-end street.

I sought counsel with a friend. Ken Leone was a Catholic priest who I knew had training and experience in spiritual matters. He said he could help me, but it would be painful. "How painful?" I asked. "For you it will be quite painful," he replied.

Shortly thereafter I was on my way to a Benedictine monastery in Tulsa, Oklahoma, all arranged by my priest friend. Ahead of me lay two weeks of retreat, silence, solitude, Scripture reading, worship, and prayer. As a Christian activist (that is, someone whose identity was tied into my activity and accomplishment) and an organizational head, I found this to be most difficult, especially the isolation factor. And besides, didn't these sisters in this little monastery realize who was living in one of their huts? (Of course they did—another Protestant activist!)

None of the sisters ever asked me what I did for my life-work. I found this to be both irritating and painful. I needed to tell them that I was the President of a large youth organization, so they would be properly impressed. As the days in silence and worship continued I began to understand something I had never realized about myself. *So much of my self-worth was tied to my performance. Things I did in ministry had become more important to me than who I was before God as his child, and as a follower of Jesus.*

Thankfully, Sister Pascaline, who led the monastery, was quite experienced in dealing with Protestant Christian activist leaders and pastors, having counseled many of them over the years. Carefully and lovingly she helped me to see myself in the presence of Jesus. During those days I heard Jesus ask within my spirit, "Do you love me?" It was only when I could say with Peter, as recorded in John 21:15–17, "Yes. Lord, you know I love you!" that Jesus could say, "Feed my sheep!"

In one startling moment I realized the true motivation for Christian ministry. It is THE LOVE OF JESUS! My "feeding sheep," my ministry in Young Life, must flow spontaneously out of that love for me and through me!

And now, for whatever time remains in our lives, Claudia and I wish to encourage people in ministries like Young Life, many who are Christian activists, so that they will always continue their inner journeys with Jesus. All authentic Christian activity must flow out of prayer. This is an imperative for any follower of our Lord!

How do we develop a dependence upon our Lord, so that we become more confident that we are following his will? When we go to kids, will we go out of a vital personal intimacy with Jesus? What will be our motivation and our strength?

Volumes have been written on the "spiritual disciplines." I shall refer to some of these writers in my letters. Most of them agree that spirituality is not something that happens automatically within the believer. Rather, it is a personal, inner-relationship with God that flourishes only as we come face to face each day with him in prayer. We learn to listen to his voice, and to enjoy his presence.

Of course I am continually learning this lesson. At times the ego gets in the way. Performance issues may still have their way. But I know the answers now.

As amazing as it may seem, Jesus wishes to continue the "Incarnation event" in his followers. He will live out his life in and through each of us, in our Young Life ministries, or anywhere else.

Remember the great words of promise in 2 Corinthians 3:18—"And we, who with unveiled faces all reflect the Lord's glory, are being transformed into his likeness with ever-increasing glory, which comes from the Lord, who is the Spirit." I want to keep on learning to let go, to abandon myself, to let God transform me in any way he chooses to reflect his glory. This is my prayer for all of us, in whatever calling we find ourselves. Simply, may we be people who reflect Jesus in the hurting world around us! May we be people of prayer, out of which all energy, activity, and accomplishment flows!

In his book, *The Pursuit of God*, A. W. Tozer describes how the Holy Spirit does his mysterious work within us, often as he uses the words of Scripture. "It is important that we get still to wait on God. Then if we will we may draw near to God and begin to hear him speak to us in our hearts. First a sound as of a Presence walking in the garden, then a voice more intelligible but still far from clear. Then the happy moment when the Spirit begins to speak—warm and intimate and clear as the word of a dear friend." It is then that we are able to minister most effectively in Young Life, or anywhere else we are called.

The areas of the spiritual experience which we will consider in these letters are:

- Adoration and Praise

- Confession, Intercession, and Petition

- Solitude, Silence, and the Jesus Prayer

- Praying the Scriptures

Please know that we cannot in a few letters cover completely the subject of spiritual formation. I encourage you to read and to pray, and in future years to devote yourself to this most-important pursuit in your life. It is all about getting to know who Jesus is, and who we are.

Young Life was born in prayer. Jim Rayburn and the handful of early staff realized that a mission with young people could only survive and be effective if it was rooted in prayer. I grew up in this atmosphere, and I am most grateful for such an invaluable learning experience.

As a leader you are called to build relationships with young people, but essentially to be a person who allows the Holy Spirit to work in and through you. This is where life-transforming, eternal power resides. Jesus said, "Apart from me you can do nothing" (John 15:5).

Remember his final words, recorded in Acts 1:8, "But you will receive power when the Holy Spirit comes on you; and you will be my witnesses in Jerusalem, and in all Judea and Samaria, and to the ends of the earth." What an awesome gift has been given to us—to give the Bread of Life to a hungry world!

— Letter 34 —

Adoration and Praise

Dear Leader,

There are two spiritual disciplines which usually are mentioned together in most written reflections. They are the disciplines of adoration and praise. In some ways these disciplines are similar but there are important distinctions between them as well.

Down through Christian history many hymns have been written which remind us of these disciplines. We all remember the words of the Christmas carol, "O come let us *adore* him … Christ the Lord." And we remember the doxology, "*Praise* God from whom all blessings flow …"

Let's not make too radical a distinction between adoration and praise; it is not necessary to do so. They are on the same wavelength. But there is a difference: in adoration we love God simply for who he is; in praise we love God for what he has done. I know it may be hard to separate the person of God from the works of God, but that is what we are dealing with here. It is two sides of the same wonderful truth.

We need both disciplines in our lives. We need those times when we praise the Lord for specific blessings, like after a good club meeting, or when a young person opens his or her life to Jesus, or when a contribution is received from a donor. And we need also those times when we sit in awe and wonder, in adoration, simply reflecting on who God is and his attributes.

When I was young and on staff, Jim took a handful of us on a very difficult climb up the Maroon Bells, one of Colorado's 14,000-foot peaks. At one point on the climb we were exposed to rock formations which seemed impossible to scale. We had gotten off course from the recommended and usual route for climbing this mountain. Hours went by as we picked our way up sheer rock outcroppings. Through the grace of God we made it to the top. The first thing we did was to have a prayer time. It was full of praise. God had protected us and given us the strength to make the climb. Then for what seemed like an hour we simply sat together in silence on that mountain peak, drinking in the awesome view of the Continental Divide, and experiencing the presence of our Lord. Not a word was spoken. In a new way we had become aware of who God is in his person, and we were in awe. Our praise for safety on the climb transitioned into adoration as we sat in the presence of the Creator.

We learn the most about adoration and praise when we read the Psalms. In Psalm 51:15 we hear the ultimate desire of David as he calls out to the Father, "O LORD, open my lips, and my mouth will declare your praise." And the shortest psalm in the Bible, only two verses long, summarizes beautifully the heart's desire of the psalmist: "Praise the Lord, all you nations; praise him all you peoples. For great is his love toward us, and the faithfulness of the Lord endures forever. PRAISE THE LORD!" (Psalm 117)

In Campaigners as a high school student, I discovered Psalm 117, and I memorized it so I could say to the group that I knew an entire psalm by heart. It was a lousy motive for Scripture memory, and not nearly as funny as I thought. But God had the last laugh and this psalm has been a wonderful blessing in my life ever since. He must have a great sense of humor!

Most of you reading these letters are younger, and many are in the prime of life, pursuing God's call for you. But some of us are older, and are in a period of reflection and recollection, when we look back upon many years of life and service. I do not regret where I am these days as one in the "older category." Sure, I wish I would have done some things differently, but I know I must not beat up on myself with regrets over past shortcomings. I wake up each day with the realization that I am still alive, and the Father has given to me another day to live for Jesus.

Often I begin the day at sunrise, sitting in our breakfast room, or on our back deck, drinking in the beauty of a Colorado morning. Soon the birds arrive at our feeders—all kinds of birds—and they too are welcoming the new day. I am experiencing what Maltbie Babcock in the late 1800s wrote about in his hymn, *This Is My Father's World*. "All nature sings and round me rings the music of the spheres."

I may not be able to explain all that adoration and praise means theologically, but I know why in the days ahead I wish always to experience these wonderful spiritual disciplines.

O COME LET US ADORE HIM!

As ever,

Mitch

Confession, Intercession, and Petition

Dear Leader,

As I promised, we shall be looking at certain spiritual disciplines which all believers may practice in order to grow in their relationship with God. These are not sure-fire formulas for successful Christian living, but rather are ways to position ourselves before the One who loves us dearly, and who wishes to express that love through his Spirit within us.

As a leader of young people your ministry will be enhanced as you engage in these disciplines. But there is a greater reason for following them. These spiritual disciplines help us to know Jesus more intimately.

Today we look at the disciplines of confession, intercession, and petition. Each of these is a means for us in prayer, and is a part of the spiritual journey.

The Discipline of Confession. One of the first verses I memorized in my high school Campaigners group was 1 John 1:9—"If we confess our sins, he is faithful and just to forgive us our sins and cleanse us from all unrighteousness." Confession, that is, saying to the Lord, "Truly I am sorry, I seek your forgiveness," is an essential daily practice. The theology in all of this is important. Jesus accomplished forgiveness for the entire world through his death upon the cross. It is with the awareness of his eternal sacrifice that we come to the Father in honesty and faith to confess our shortcomings. We do not beg for forgiveness, knowing that forgiveness has already been accomplished. But rather, we acknowledge gratefully his sacrifice for us and thank him for all that this forgiveness means in the present moment and in each day of our lives. This is the way of thankful confession.

Dietrich Bonhoeffer, the great German theologian and author, wrote in *Life Together*, "Confession as a pious work is an invention of the devil. It is only God's offer of grace, help, and forgiveness that could make us dare to enter the abyss of confession. We can confess solely for the sake of the promise of absolution. Confession as routine duty is spiritual death; confession in reliance upon the promise is life." Let us not do our confession as some necessary ritual, but as the honest and necessary response of our hearts toward a loving and forgiving God.

Pat Evans, one of my notorious fellow high school Work Crew members at Star Ranch in Colorado in the 1940s, described the forgiveness of Jesus that he was experiencing as, "I feel like I've had a bath on the inside!" Not a bad description (and of course we need to bathe regularly—both physically and spiritually!).

The Discipline of Intercession. James 5:16 says, "Confess your sins to each other and pray for each other so that you may be healed. The prayer of a righteous man is powerful and effective." How important it is for Young Life leaders to pray for one another, and also to pray for all believers in the Church around the world that they might be encouraged in their spiritual journeys and effective in their proclamation of the gospel!

Some believers have found it helpful to keep a prayer list of people for whom they wish to pray regularly. I encourage this discipline if it fits your lifestyle. (I remember what it felt like one day when I was in high school to sneak a look at Jim Rayburn's prayer journal, and there was my name close to the top of the list of people he prayed for each day! What a joy it was to know that this dedicated and gifted man loved me enough to pray for me each day!)

Henri Nouwen in his book, *The Way of the Heart*, offered this insight about intercession: "When we say to people, 'I will pray for you,' we make a very important commitment. The sad thing is that this remark often remains nothing but a well-meant expression of concern." Too often I am afraid we make these statements to others as appropriate conversation, or nice thoughts, rather than real commitments to intercession. Let us not tell people we are praying for them if really we are not.

Once again, we learn from the example of our Savior. Hebrews 7:25 describes the intercessory work of Jesus, "He always lives to intercede for them." It is hard to describe the feelings of awe and gratitude I have as I write this letter to you. *Jesus prays for us constantly!* How much more, then, should we be praying for one another!

The Discipline of Petition. The Apostle Paul writes to the Philippians in 4:6: "Do not be anxious about anything, but in everything, by prayer and petition, with thanksgiving, present your requests to God. And the peace of God, which transcends all understanding, will guard your hearts and your minds in

Christ Jesus." What a fabulous promise for the Young Life leader! God will guard your heart and mind!

I know there are things about being a leader which may cause anxiety. Having been a club leader and staff person for over fifty years I know the feelings of anxiety and doubt. Please take Paul's words to heart. They are golden!

James Stewart, the great theologian and author, many years ago said some important things about petitionary prayer. "There is a dangerous tendency today, even among good Christian people, to speak disparagingly of petitionary prayer and to say that asking for definite things from God is prayer of such a rudimentary and childish form that it ought to have no place in the religion of the mature and fully developed believer. This we must quite definitely deny. The idea that it is expedient to outgrow petitionary prayer goes to pieces on one clear fact—Jesus never outgrew it" (*Life and Teaching of Jesus Christ*).

Let us come then with thanksgiving, bringing our petitions to his throne of grace!

Sincerely in Christ,

Mitch

— Letter 36 —

Solitude, Silence, and the "Jesus Prayer"

Dear Young Life Leader,

Let's look together at three disciplines for the inner life – solitude, silence, and the "Jesus Prayer." Once again, we are entering "uncharted waters" for many Young Life leaders. Solitude and silence seem distant from the atmosphere of the teenage culture, and the Jesus Prayer may not be on our radar screen at all. I will make the rather dogmatic assertion that each of these spiritual disciplines may in fact be essential for us as leaders of young people.

Okay, let's start with *solitude*. Does a Young Life leader really need alone-time? In the performance of our ministry we must be "relational people," building bridges of friendship with all sorts of needy kids, and relating with our leadership team and other associates in ministry. Where does solitude fit in with all of that energy and activity?

I can't speak for you, your schedule, or your priorities. That is your business. But I can call your attention to the life of Jesus, for whom solitude was essential and frequent. Jesus often went away to a quiet place to be alone with his Father. If it was that important for the Son of God to seek the solitude of prayer, how much more for us as created beings, who are dependent upon God for life itself!

Tilden Edwards, a great teacher of spiritual formation, with whom Claudia and I studied years ago, said in his book, *Spiritual Friend*, "There was one other dimension of the rhythm of Jesus: solitude. Jesus' culminating preparation for his ministry was alone, in the wilderness ..." Solitude for Jesus was an imperative. It needs to be for us as well.

Do you have a quiet place to which you can go to be alone with the Lord? This may not be easy to find in your living situation. Pray about this matter. The Lord will help you to find that place of quiet. Maybe the hardest thing for you will be turning off your cell phone, computer, and other electronic devices. This is imperative, and may require strict discipline on your part. Our modern electronic culture can be devastating to any who wish to hear the "still, small voice" of the Lord in solitude and prayer.

Now let us look at *silence*. Again, we are considering a subject that may seem contradictory to the Young Life ethos. It was a radical change for us when years ago we instituted a period of twenty minutes for an entire camp to be silent following the message of Jesus and his death upon the cross. But how powerful that has been for campers! So many have made faith commitments during that time of silence!

Psalm 46:10 is quite clear in its admonition. "Be still, and know that I am God." People often come to faith when there is a release from the noise and distractions of their world, and there is a growing awareness of a loving God. Their stillness leads to knowledge.

Thomas Merton, in *Thoughts in Solitude*, says these helpful words: "Silence, then, belongs to the substance of sanity. In silence and hope are formed the strength of the Saints" (cf. Isaiah 30:15).

We should welcome silence both in mind and in spirit so that we may hear God's voice. This will take practice. Ours is a verbal society, and certainly Young Life is in that social current. We wish to be effective communicators of the gospel, but that does not mean we must talk all the time. When we give a message in club or camp there needs to be a sense that the message is from God, who is not frantic or in a great hurry. Use the pause effectively in your messages. It may be more powerful than saying a bunch more words.

Silence is our friend and we may experience the depth of our friendship each day. BE STILL AND KNOW THAT I AM GOD!

Now let us consider *the Jesus Prayer*. It is believed that this spiritual discipline has its roots in Russia, when an anonymous pilgrim went on a journey among spiritual fathers searching for the meaning of the Scripture, "Pray without ceasing" (1 Thessalonians 5:17, ESV). The Jesus Prayer is a prayer that may be repeated by followers of Jesus as that "prayer without ceasing."

The usual wording of the prayer is, "Lord Jesus Christ, Son of God, have mercy on me, a sinner." We recognize these words as coming from a tax collector who met Jesus and had his life changed radically (Luke 18:13).

For many believers the Jesus Prayer becomes that which spiritual directors refer to as our "prayer word." We may repeat it silently, over and over, as we continue through each day. I began praying this "prayer word" many years ago, and now I find myself praying it silently dozens of times each day. I find that it has a settling effect upon my life and is a wonderful reminder of the presence of Jesus at all times.

One helpful practice may be to coordinate this prayer with the rhythm of our breathing. We breathe in while saying silently the words, "Lord Jesus Christ, Son of God," and we breathe out while saying silently the words, "have mercy on me, a sinner."

Some may find repetition in prayer to be distracting. For the first several months of praying with this "prayer word" I was one of those persons. Now it has become a part of my everyday experience of God's presence throughout the day, and at night as well.

Please know that there is not one right way to pray. God will lead you in your prayer journey. He knows you intimately and wishes to give himself to you in the wonderful mystery of his presence.

God bless you in your journey of prayer!

Mitch

Lectio Divina

Dear Leader,

Many years ago Claudia and I were introduced to the Benedictine discipline of *Lectio Divina*, or "praying the Scriptures." We continue to teach this discipline with Young Life leaders and other groups. Especially is Lectio good for activists because it encourages us in our inner journeys with Jesus, helping us to be more reflective in that journey, and it conditions us to listen to Jesus.

To lay biblical groundwork for the subject of this letter, please go with me to the wonderful transfiguration event of our Lord Jesus, described in Luke 9:28–36. This is one of my very favorite stories of Jesus with his disciples, and it continues to teach us so much in today's culture of ministry.

> About eight days after Jesus said this, he took Peter, John and James with him and went up onto a mountain to pray. As he was praying, the appearance of his face changed, and his clothes became as bright as a flash of lightning. Two men, Moses and Elijah,

appeared in glorious splendor, talking with Jesus. They spoke about his departure, which he was about to bring to fulfillment at Jerusalem. Peter and his companions were very sleepy, but when they became fully awake, they saw his glory and the two men standing with him. As the men were leaving Jesus, Peter said to him, 'Master, it is good for us to be here. Let us put up three shelters—one for you, one for Moses and one for Elijah.' (He did not know what he was saying.)

While he was speaking, a cloud appeared and enveloped them, and they were afraid as they entered the cloud. A voice came from the cloud, saying, 'This is my Son, whom I have chosen; *listen to him*.' When the voice had spoken, they found that Jesus was alone. The disciples kept this to themselves, and told no one at that time what they had seen [emphasis added].

When we look at this remarkable experience on the mountain with Jesus and a few of his disciples we learn so much about God the Father, about Jesus the Son, and about ourselves as his followers. I don't know how many times I have spoken with various groups and explored the timeless truths of this transfiguration account. The number of times is quite large, but may we go there again to discover the Father's wishes for us as his disciples, and as leaders of young people?

Jesus took three of his disciples with him up the mountain to pray. Prayer was central in his ministry. Obviously, the most important thing in the life of our Lord was his relationship with his Father. This time he took with him Peter, John, and James.

What a privilege for these men to have such an intimate experience with him! The wonderful reality is that we also may have our own intimate prayer experience with Jesus each day. Is it happening in your life, or does activity crowd out those invaluable prayer times? Above anything else, my highest wish for you as a leader is that you be a person of prayer and intimacy with Jesus!

As Jesus was praying, something remarkable happened. His appearance changed and his clothes became exceptionally bright, like lightning. And now we witness one of the rare times when we hear the audible voice of God the Father. (Another time this occurred was during the baptism of Jesus.)

Two men, Moses and Elijah, appear in glorious splendor. We remember that Moses is the great lawgiver, and Elijah the great prophet. The law and the prophets are joined together in this historic moment. The two men are talking with Jesus about his "departure" which is soon to occur in Jerusalem. They are referring to his forthcoming sacrifice upon the cross—his departure through pain, suffering, and death. In essence they are encouraging him to "Go on! You are headed in the right direction!" How much it must have meant to Jesus to receive this affirmation and encouragement from these two servants of his!

Peter and his companions are very sleepy as all of this is happening. It is not the first time the disciples are sleeping through important moments. But let's not be too hard on them. How many times have we "slept" through occasions and periods of our lives, and have missed the important messages our Lord wishes to give to us?

The disciples wake up to see the glory of Jesus and the two men standing with him. Somehow it is given to them to know who these men are, and of course they are astonished. Always the expressive, Peter blurts out something about building monuments to Moses, Elijah, and Jesus. This is not his greatest moment! (The King James Version of the Bible says, "He wist not what to say ..." I think that if ever we "wist not what to say," we should keep our mouths shut, don't you?)

And now a heavy cloud envelops them all. It is a frightening moment when out of the cloud a voice is heard, "This is my son, whom I have chosen. Listen to him!" When the voice had spoken they find that Jesus is alone.

So what does it all mean for us today? We hear one clear command from God the Father, *"Listen to him!"* We don't hear the Father saying, "Do great things for him," or "Build huge organizations for him." More than anything else it seems obvious that the Father wishes for us to listen to his Son, Jesus Christ! That of course leads us to the question of "How do we listen to Jesus?"

The ways for listening are many. We listen to Jesus in the Scriptures, in our prayer experiences, in the words of his followers, in the events of history, in the gathering of his Church, and in all of creation.

Quite a few leaders I have met know very little about the spiritual discipline of "contemplation." It sounds rather heavy, and usually they associate it with the monastic life. Many monks and sisters live in residences where they exist in an atmosphere of contemplation. These places seem about as far as one can get from the schedule and "feel" of a Young Life camp!

I wish to make the seemingly absurd suggestion that the most effective youth leaders may in fact be contemplatives. The Young Life ethos, and the atmosphere of youth leadership in general, is not contrary to the contemplative lifestyle. One spiritual director, Thelma Hall, in her wonderful book, *Too Deep For Words,* writes, "Without always being able to explain or define it, what many feel called to is to become 'contemplatives in action.' This is not an impossible ideal for today's committed Christian. Indeed, it may well be the new vocation of a great number of lay-people, whatever their state in life. For there is nothing mutually exclusive between the two terms, 'contemplation' and 'action'; they are in fact complementary."

Certainly we see contemplation in the life of Jesus, who is eternity's supreme activist. Thelma Hall continues, "In Jesus' life prayer and action follow one another in a rhythm which seems as constant as the inhaling and exhaling of breathing." Jesus spent nights in prayer with the Father. He went into the hills alone to pray. Yet, no person has accomplished so much in one active life as did Jesus. When we hear his final words upon the cross, "It is finished," we know he has just completed the bridge to heaven for all of humankind. What could be more significant or productive!

Lectio Divina is a spiritual discipline which enables believers to experience God in his eternal presence. It is a form of prayer which may be used in approaching any text of Scripture. It is not a Bible study method. Rather, in this discipline we are praying the Scriptures, and always there are contemplative times when we sit in silence, not analyzing the words or forming interpretations. These are times simply for being in the Father's presence. This is the "prayer that is without words." In our verbal society it is a new experience for many followers of Jesus.

Lectio Divina may be experienced by one person alone or in a small group. For instance, the group may consist of other leaders, a camp team, an area committee, or other regular gatherings of Young Life people. You will need to allow thirty minutes to an hour for this prayer experience. We should never feel rushed.

When we do Lectio alone it is important to keep a journal of our responses. When we meet in a small group we share briefly with the group our insights and discoveries. I shall describe how this discipline might flow with the small group. (Please make appropriate modifications when you are practicing Lectio alone.)

Spiritual directors teach that there are various rhythms we experience in Lectio Divina. Thelma Hall lists four such rhythms, or steps, for this prayer journey. The following is a brief summary of her teaching.

Step One: *Lectio: Reading and listening to the Word of God*

The first step is *Lectio*, or reading. It is not ordinary reading. We are approaching the divine words of Scripture. This is holy ground. Contrary to much of our prayer experience, we come mostly to "listen" and to "hear," and not so much to "speak." We tune our hearts to the Speaker, as the Father instructed the disciples on the Mount of Transfiguration.

We may choose any passage of Scripture for this prayer experience, but as a general rule it should be short enough not to feel overwhelmed with content. Actually, it is even possible to practice Lectio with only one or two verses. A desired length might be five to fifteen verses, but we must not be rigid concerning this matter of length. Sometimes we may look at a biblical story. Other times it may be a teaching passage or a psalm.

When we practice Lectio with a small group we should have one person read the chosen text aloud. It is not necessary for others to follow along in their Bibles. In fact this is not recommended. Rather, each one sits quietly and reflectively listening to the Word of God as it is read.

In the first reading each person listens for any word or phrase that stands out for them. This word or phrase seems to rise from the page, sinking into one's mind and heart. Do not analyze it or develop it in any way. Simply be aware of this word or phrase and hold it in your memory. It is a gift to you from God, even though you may not understand at this time why it is given.

Now we sit briefly for a period of silence to call upon the divine interpreter, the Holy Spirit, to engage our hearts and minds with our God.

Ask the group what word or phrase was given to each of them. Each person simply reports his or her word or phrase with no commentary or application.

Step Two: *Meditatio: Reflecting on the Word of God*

The second step is *meditatio,* or reflecting on the Word. Here we begin to learn who God really is for us in this moment.

Read the same text again. This time each person seeks the Lord in the reading with the questions, "What do I see? What do I hear? What do I feel?"

Sit for a period of silence. Then each person reports briefly what he or she saw, heard, or felt in the reading.

Step Three: *Oratio: The Word touches the heart*

The third step is *oratio*, the deepest center, or the prayer of the heart.

Read the same text again. This time each person seeks the Lord with questions such as, "Where are you taking me, Lord?" "What do you wish for me to believe, to do, or possibly to change?" Sit for a period of silence and then each person may share whatever he or she wishes concerning that which was given to him or her.

Step Four: *Contemplatio: Silent reflection*

The fourth step is *contemplatio,* when we are simply being, or abiding, in God's presence. We have no agenda, words, or formed prayer.

Read the same text again. Sit together in silent reflection, breathing in the presence of the Lord.

To conclude the session, the group may repeat together the Lord's Prayer.

May God bless you in this wonderful prayer journey!

As ever,

Mitch

Acknowledgments

I wish to thank several people for their encouragement, prodding, and continuing optimism toward the writing of this book.

Especially, I thank Claudia, my wonderful wife, who believed in me and gave most helpful reflections on each letter.

And thanks to Ken Knipp, Randy Jackson, Ken Tankersley, and Tom Hammon, friends in Young Life leadership positions who have kept me in the game and enabled me to continue making some contribution to the mission I love.

And thanks to my kids, Tucker, Tammy, and Tim, who often have asked, "How's the book coming, Dad?"

And finally, my appreciation for my editor and publisher, Kit Sublett, who has been most patient and encouraging in this undertaking.

— Colophon —

Main body composed in Arno Pro 11/13.5. Arno Pro, named after the Arno River in Florence, was designed by Robert Slimbach. Titles composed in Eaglefeather, a font based on the distinctive handwriting of the architect Frank Lloyd Wright. Cover designed by Stephanie W. Dicken.

You might also enjoy—

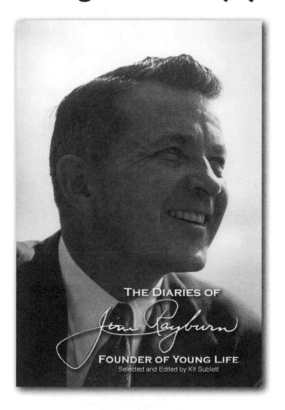

The Diaries of Jim Rayburn
ISBN 978-0-9758577-7-9

Jim Rayburn was the founder of Young Life
and one of the great men of faith of the 20th
century. His journals recount his struggles
and triumphs, making a fascinating read.

For more information, please visit
whitecapsmedia.com